GOOD FRIENDS
ARE HARD TO FIND

GOOD FRIENDS
ARE HARD TO FIND

HELP YOUR CHILD
FIND, MAKE AND KEEP FRIENDS

Fred Frankel, PH.D.
Illustrations by Barry Wetmore

Perspective Publishing
Los Angeles

Library of Congress Catalogue Card Number 96-9753
ISBN: 0-9622036-7-X

Published by Perspective Publishing, Inc., 50 S. DeLacey Ave.
#201, Pasadena, CA 91105, 818-440-9635

Additional copies of this book may be ordered by calling toll free
1-800-330-5851

Library of Congress Cataloging-in-Publication Data

Frankel, Fred H.
    Good Friends are hard to find: help your child find, make,
and keep friends / Fred Frankel ; illustrations by Barry
Wetmore.
        p.   cm.
    Includes bibliographical references and index.
    ISBN 0-9622036-7-X
    1. Friendship in children.   Social skills in children.
I. Title.
HQ784.F7F73   1996
302'.34'083—dc20   96-9753
                                                  CIP

Illustrations by Barry Wetmore
Back cover photo by Lucinda Frankel
Printed in the United States of America
First Edition

To Lucinda and Seth, my inspirations.

ACKNOWLEDGMENTS

I am thankful for being in the right place at the right time. I am greatly indebted to Bob Myatt, Ph.D. who brought his expertise from doctoral work on children's social skills at the University of Mississippi. Through helping my wife raise our child and through the success of the program Bob Myatt and I developed at UCLA, I met many parents and children. (I have changed names and other identifying details to protect confidentiality.) The help and encouragement of Linda Pillsbury and Cynthia Whitham, L.C.S.W. turned my experiences into this book.

I am also indebted to the following people for their help: Sue Ann Tanzer Roberts and her daughters Heather and Anna; Rhonda Finehout; Carole Hart; Karen Hart and her daughters Eliza and Alexa; Leah and Allison Pillsbury; Melanie d'Avis and her daughter Nicole; and Diann Poulin. I would also like to thank Suzanne Levanas, L.C.S.W. and the mothers who read an early draft of this book, giving me many helpful comments: Emily O'Connell, Carol Glazer, Valerie Cummings, Nan Freitas, Marjorie Oronella, Sarah Moaba, Jan Dockendorf, and Sandra Sloane.

CONTENTS

INTRODUCTION

When I began my clinical practice in the mid 1980's, a lot of the families coming to me for treatment had children with friendship problems. Conventional treatments (individual, group and family therapy) are not effective with these problems. I started to think about what I could do to help. In 1990, my son was five years old and just beginning to make friends by himself. I noticed how he did this and what my wife and I had to do to keep this going. I also noticed that other parents in our neighborhood, whose children had friends, were doing pretty much the same things.

I also looked at what researchers had discovered about children's friendships. The 1980's were productive years for researchers interested in children with friendship problems. Developmental psychologists made breakthroughs. They started by asking children whom they liked and disliked playing with. They found that many children were quietly suffering from friendship problems—15% had no friends at all. They identified the things children did that led to friendship problems and what well adjusted children did in the same situations.

Some researchers had the patience (and funding) to see what happened to these children as they grew up. What they found was eye-opening: Children who had chronic difficulties making and keeping friends were more likely to drop out of school and have drug problems in adolescence. Children who did not have a best friend outside the family (brother and sister don't count here) grew up to be lonely young adults. They found that close friends teach

each other social grace and how to solve disagreements. Close friends support each other in stressful times and help each other to look beyond their own needs and become sensitive to others.

I put the research together with the practical experiences my wife and I were having and developed the UCLA Social Skills Training Program with Bob Myatt. This program helps children make friends.

I find that children with friendship problems come from all types of families. These problems are not a sign of poor parenting. Some parents who came to me had children with simple problems. Sometimes I could give parents simple advice over the telephone. When I did this, they would call me back the next week to thank me. Many children had a once in a while problem, like losing a friend or choosing a friend unwisely. I could help these parents with a brief consultation.

Some parents had children who had trouble picking up social cues. These children had trouble making friends or having a best friend and sometimes would earn a bad reputation among their peers. We have helped over 300 of these children and their parents in our Making and Keeping Friends classes. The results of our clinical trials were gratifying: Improvement on our five outcome measures ranged from 82-91% of children. Children in our classes with Attention-Deficit/Hyperactivity Disorder (ADHD, see Chapter 24) who were taking Ritalin or a similar medication showed improvement on four of five measures at the same level as the children without ADHD.

I can help only a limited number of parents and children through my clinical practice. Many parents who contact me need more than I have time to give on the phone but less than a 12 week class. I looked around for a book to recommend to help these parents, but couldn't find anything. That's why I wrote this book.

This book is based on our program at UCLA. In the last six years of this program, I learned that the more parents know about how they can help their child, the better the children's social behavior becomes at home and in school.

Our most important finding has been that one-on-one play dates are the best way to build close friendships. I mean by a one-on-one play date that your child invites only one guest over and plays with her in private. Your child is completely responsible for the entertainment. You are responsible for transportation, snacks and usually little else. One-on-one play dates are the only time when children can get to know each other intimately without interruption. One-on-one play dates let your child maintain a continuing relationship with her friends. Some parents tell me that they don't need to make play dates. They feel their child sees enough children during the day at school. Besides, it takes a lot of effort to schedule play dates. I think they're making a big mistake.

Studies show that between 55 and 90 percent of parents today are arranging play dates for their children. One-on-one play dates enhance your child's self-esteem. When you arrange a one-on-one play date for your child, you make her feel special. Your child sees that another child likes her enough to want to play exclusively with her. What's more, she sees it's important to you and lots of fun for her. If all goes well, you notice the warm glow she has after the play date.

I have organized this book into step by step plans that address common friendship issues. You don't need to read this book cover to cover. Just focus on the areas in which your child needs help, solving one problem at a time. I show you the most important rules to teach your child and which problems to solve first. I have made the rules easy for you to teach to your child. I have organized each chapter into four sections:

1. THE PROBLEM describes specific problems helped by the chapter.

2. BACKGROUND helps you to understand causes and solutions of each problem.

3. SOLVING THE PROBLEM gives you step-by-step instructions to practice with your child.

4. THE NEXT STEP tells you which problem to solve next and which chapters to read.

What this book will not help

This book will not help children handle unavoidable times when they are required to be together with other children they do not like (for example, family reunions, visiting relatives, or entertaining children of our adult friends). To cope with these times, we just need to think more about what friendship is:

Friendship is a mutual relationship formed with affection and commitment between people who consider themselves equals.

We shouldn't expect our children to be friends with other children we require them to be with. We should expect them to be civil. This book will not help our child get along better with us. Children should respect and obey their parents and there are many good books written about this. This book will not help the child with autism, who is in his own world, or the child with general delays in learning, motor and social behavior. These children need intensive programs offered by psychologists and recreational therapists.

The children I see improve the most have parents who discuss problems with them and know how to help. You are the best person to help your child solve friendship problems. So don't let these problems baffle you. If you follow the steps in this book, and your child tries what you suggest, your child will have richer social experiences.

PART I: FINDING FRIENDS

Even if his nose is always buried in a book or her days are so packed with activities that there's no time—your child needs friends. And you CAN help find them.

1
MAKING TIME FOR FRIENDS

THE PROBLEM:

I'm not sure my child has the time to have friends, what with homework and all of the activities she's in. What can I do?

BACKGROUND: Too busy to have friends?

Our life-styles leave children less play time

Our modern life-styles pull our children away from friendships. Teachers have larger classes and depend more on homework to teach children. The added homework spills over into our child's afternoons and evenings. In more families, both parents work, so families spend less time together during the week. Some use weekends for family time. There is less time for everyone's friends.

We misplace our time

School-aged children average 27 hours of TV viewing per week. That's an average—some children watch considerably more. Children are home Saturday mornings watching TV instead of playing with each other. Many parents tell me they think this is harmless. After all, TV is everywhere in American culture. But I feel we are sacrificing companionship for entertainment.

We give away our time.
Parents tell me they put their child in many different structured activities—soccer, scouts, music lessons, computer class, karate. These activities can effectively fill up their child's free time without leaving time for friends.

Children need time for one-on-one play dates. These are the best way to make friends. Classes, sports and scouts may be good ways to meet other children, but your child needs enough open time for one or two play dates per week of at least two hours each (kindergarten and first graders start out with shorter play dates). You need to open up more than four hours to make your child accessible to other children's schedules. Even if both parents work, you have all day Saturday and Sunday for play dates.

SOLVING THE PROBLEM:
How to free up time for friends
Step 1: Calculate how much time your child has for close friends.

Figure out how much prime time your child currently has for one-on-one play dates. Prime time is when other children are likely to get together with your child. Include only times when:

  ◆ you are around to supervise.

  ◆ your child can see a single playmate of her choice.

  ◆ your child can play without brother or sister around.

  ◆ your child and her friend can choose what they want to play.

Here are typical times for play dates, figuring school ends at 2:30:

Prime times for play dates

Day(s)	Prime Times	Total Hours
Monday - Thursday	2:30 - 6 p.m.	14
Friday	2:30 - 7 p.m.	4 1/2
Saturday & Sunday	10 a.m. - 7 p.m.	17
TOTAL Prime time		**35 1/2**

I don't include sleep-over time (Friday and Saturday after 7:00 p.m.) as prime time. Sleep-overs are valuable for children who are becoming good friends, but not for the first few play dates.

If you and your partner both work, then you don't have Monday through Friday. This leaves only 17 hours per week of prime time. How many hours does your child have for one-on-one play dates? This needs to total at least 4 hours per week during prime time. If the total is usually less, go to Step 2.

Step 2: Drop that activity that doesn't yield friendships.

Make a list of all the activities your child has during prime time and how many hours each takes up. The next table shows a typical list for an over-scheduled child.

An over-scheduled child

Activity	Weekly time commitment
Homework	8 hours
Music lessons and practice	6 hours
Play with neighbor's child I baby-sit	2 hours
Little League games and practice	4 1/2 hours
Religious school	4 hours
Scouts	1 1/2 hours
Soccer	4 1/2 hours
Watching TV	3 hours
Origami class	2 hours
TOTAL	**35 1/2 hours**

All of this child's prime time is taken. She has no time to develop close friendships. She needs to free four hours for this essential activity. What are the things to cut back? Here are my suggestions. The first things to drop are at the top of the following list. If you can't drop them, then move down the list until you find something else to drop.

Activities to Drop

1. TV and videogames are the least necessary, waste the most time and are most easily dropped at the last minute. Schedule that play date to take the place of Saturday morning TV (the TV stays off during the play date).

2. Playing with friends of convenience (a child of your friend, relative, or neighbor, whom your child does not like) has none of the benefits of playing with a close friend. If you can arrange a play date with someone your child likes, then cancel these other commitments (a week's notice will be sufficient).

3. Teams or scouts with poor adult supervision benefit no one. Your child is better off at home than being yelled at by a coach or left to his own devices.

4. Teams or scouts outside your neighborhood that don't lead to play dates in your home.

5. Non-school instruction, such as origami, karate or art class is fun, and can be a place to meet friends, but what good is meeting friends if your child never gets to know them?

6. Duplicate team or scout activities (little league, soccer, and swim team practice are too much). Don't cut them all out, just the least productive. All you need is one of these at any given time for your child. You are not doing yourself or your child a favor by involving her in more than one of these activities at a time if she can't see friends.

The overscheduled child above has more than enough of everything—teams and classes. These activities might have been good ideas when you signed your child up, but you need to look at the total schedule at this point and set your priorities. Think about eliminating the activity that would lead to the fewest play dates. Open up blocks of time by dropping non-school classes or activities.

Step 3: Drop that activity which soaks up your time.

You can't leave play dates for someone else to supervise. You need to be there to make sure things go well. Your time is valuable and you shouldn't be spending it in activities that don't benefit you or your child.

> *Margaret is a soft-spoken, pleasant mother of eight-year-old Todd. Todd has no friends he can invite to play with. For the past two years, Margaret has put in many hours as the leader for Todd's Cub Scout den. The den has six boys other than Todd. She spends two hours each week planning her den meetings. She plans and spends the better part of one Saturday each month on a den outing. She spends one hour per month with other den leaders planning Cub Scout pack activities.*
>
> *In spite of his mother's volunteering 22 hours per month, none of the other boys make play dates with Todd. They never invite him to their birthday parties, although they occasionally talk about their parties at Cub Scout meetings in front of Todd.*

My heart went out to Margaret when she told me this story. Despite Margaret's valiant efforts (Cub Scouts wouldn't exist without parents like Margaret volunteering their time), her child is overlooked by the other children she is helping. Putting this much time into scouts keeps her from helping Todd find children who would be happy to play with him. Here are 22 hours each month that she could devote to Todd's benefit. She has three choices at this point:

1. Devote time to arranging play dates with the parents of her Cubs,

2. Look for ways to add Cubs to her den who want to play with Todd, or

3. Graciously hand over the den to another parent. She does not owe the others her time. She can tell the other parents she is too busy to continue and they have to find someone

else. She can give Todd the choice of continuing with this den, changing to another, or dropping out of scouts.

As a Cubmaster, I have seen parents take choice #3. No one blamed them—we were glad to have their help while they could give it. The other parents will take over den leadership if they care enough for scouts.

Step 4: Make that car pool work for you and your child.

Not only do car pools save time, they can also help your child meet others her age who live close by. The common destination gives them something to talk about; riding in the car (with the radio off) gives them time to talk. Arranging play dates becomes much easier. For example, Zacky's and Clark's moms have car pooled with each other to get their boys to school. Here's how easily they arrange a play date:

Zacky's Mom: Zacky would like to know if Clark can come over
to our house this Friday.

Clark's Mom: Clark's been asking to play with Zacky, so that
would be fine.

Zacky's Mom: How about if I just take them over to our house
after school when I pick them up?

Clark's Mom: That will be fine.

But car pools can sometimes work against having friends:

*Paula and Joanne live within two blocks of each other
and are good friends. Their sons attend first grade at the
same private school across town, so they have arranged a
car pool to school. Joanne's son behaves poorly at Paula's
house, in the car, and at school. Paula's son does not like to
play with this boy, but he does anyway since he doesn't
have any other choices.*

Although Joanne and Paula are friends, the two boys are not. They are forced to be together in the car. They have play dates with each other out of desperation. I am concerned that this is preventing other relationships from sprouting. Suppose there is a boy in the area that Paula's son likes and who attends this school. Changing car pools or adding him to the car pool would give Paula's son a more suitable child to play with. Some tips on forming car pools:

- ◆ Don't make them permanent. Set them up as temporary, so that if you need to change them, no one's feelings will be hurt.

- ◆ Set them up so they save you time (but also do your share of the driving).

- ◆ Turn a ride home into a play date. Arrange play dates at pick up or drop off times to save additional time. The other parent can do the same on a day she drives.

THE NEXT STEP:

You have made changes you have wanted to make. You and your child now have more time to devote to the serious business of making friends. If your child has children to invite over, read Chapters 9 and 10 before you make your next play date. If your child spends too much time playing by himself or watching TV, read Chapter 2. If your child has trouble meeting new friends, read Chapters 5 and 6.

2
CURBING INTERESTS THAT PREVENT FRIENDSHIPS

THE PROBLEM:

My child likes to watch TV when his friends come over. Should I allow this?

My child frequently prefers playing by herself when her guest is over. What can I do?

Should I worry about my child's obsession with a toy?

BACKGROUND:
Interests which interfere with friendships

Certain recreational activities, especially TV and videogames—if carried to an extreme—rob your child of friends and interfere with play dates. These activities:

- ◆ make it hard to talk to others while they are on.

- ◆ needlessly steal time away from playing with friends.

- ◆ rob your child of the energy or desire to play with others.

- ◆ are done just as well, or better, when your child is alone.

Too hooked to have friends

Many parents use TV and videogames for baby-sitting while they get other things done. Occasional use of this captivating entertainment is relatively harmless, but some children wind up glued to TV and videogames for long periods of time.

Nine-year-old Jeremy spends much of his free time watching TV or playing videogames. He doesn't know how to play any board games or the games other boys are playing at recess. He shows little interest in sports. He has no toys at home that are interesting to other children his age. One time Michael, also age nine, came over to his house to play. They spent the whole time watching TV, barely saying a word to each other.

After the play date, Michael told his parents he was bored. Michael declines invitations to come back.

Jeremy's interest in TV has blocked his chances of being friends with Michael. Michael is a people person, the kind of friend who would be valuable for Jeremy to have. The fact that Jeremy would ignore him for two hours is a sad commentary on Jeremy's current priorities. It is difficult to get Jeremy to stop being hooked on TV.

Children need to learn how to have fun, talk, and solve problems with other children. Watching TV together with others or playing videogames for most of a play date prevents this, since the children learn little about each other.

Why is Jeremy so interested in TV to the exclusion of anything else? Is it due to a lack of interactive activities, a bad habit, or an addiction?

Too much passion for the toy, too little regard for the friend

TV addiction is easy to detect. Another type of addiction that is harmful to friendships is more difficult to spot. It's when children focus upon a game or toy, getting overly excited and losing sight of why another child is with them to play.

Natalie is seven years old and an avid collector of Barbie dolls. She plays with them by herself for hours at home and in after-school care. When she invites Leah over to play, she insists on playing Barbies and dictating to Leah how she plays with them. Leah gets tired of this after 45 minutes and finds a puzzle to put together. Natalie continues to play by herself, not noticing that Leah is no longer playing with her.

Barbies interest many seven-year-old girls. However, Natalie is so interested in Barbies that she no longer cares about her friend and what her friend wants to play.

Videogames interest many boys. When this is all they want to do with friends, then it is interfering with their ability to build deeper friendships. You can help the guest and the host by restricting videogame play so that they can find out that friendship is more than competition on a videogame.

If your child has too much passion for one toy, it's time to act.

SOLVING THE PROBLEM:
Curb addictive and exclusive interests

Parents should weed out interests which are destructive to friendships and nurture interests which build friendships. I will show how to nurture friendship-building interests in the next chapter. First, you must curb TV addiction and interests that exclude other children. Here's how:

Step 1: Set and enforce a reasonable weekly schedule.

Some TV and or videogame play is acceptable—a modest amount and at the right time. At the beginning of each week, you and your child should select a reasonable menu of TV fare from the weekly TV listings (I feel that 7 hours total is enough for the week). Circle the programs you select. You and your child know what to do when your child wants to watch a TV program—if it isn't circled, it isn't watched. (Note: your child doesn't have to watch a program just because it's circled.)

Example: Dad hears TV in the adjacent room, comes in to find his son, James, watching it. He looks at the TV listings kept next to the TV and finds the program James is watching isn't circled.

Dad: Is that one of the programs we agreed you could watch?

James: I think so.

Dad: Take a look at the listing.

James: [*Sees it is not circled*] Well, I'm bored and I have nothing to do.

Dad: At 6:00 we have circled "The Wonder Years." What can you do until then?

James: I guess I can play with my Legos.

Dad: That's a good idea. Want me to help you get them out?

Step 2: Make a deal.

In Step 1 you learned how to set your child's maximum number of hours of leisure time devoted to TV. Elementary school children have more important things they have to do, like homework, which takes priority. Make a deal with your child to do what you want first, and then what he wants. Example:

Dad: Do your homework for 30 minutes, and then you can take a 10-minute break to play a videogame.

First you work, then you play. Allow your child to play videogames only after he first completes something necessary. Your child is more likely to do the important things and he will reduce videogame time. This also works well for the addictive interest:

Mom: Natalie, you need to find another toy to play with for 30 minutes before you play with your Barbies.

Natalie: But I don't like to play with anything else.

Mom: You need to give your dolls a rest and give another toy a try. What's it going to be? Roller blades? Painting?

Natalie: I'll roller blade, then.

Mom: Good, roller blade for the next 30 minutes and then you can play with Barbies.

It is now up to Mom to enforce this as a minimum time for roller blading. Natalie can't play with Barbies before 30 minutes. She need not remind Natalie if she roller blades for longer than 30 minutes, unless Natalie asks to be reminded. If Natalie stops roller blading before 30 minutes, tell her to continue with roller blades or find something else.

Step 3: Don't let an interest exclude playmates.

If your child has an interest that sometimes excludes guests when they come over to play, make a deal with your child right before the playmate comes over:

Dad: When Michael comes over, it's time to play with him, so no TV. Have Michael help you pick a game to play.

Jeremy: What if Michael wants to watch TV?

Dad: If he asks, just tell him your parents don't allow TV when guests are over.

Natalie's mother makes a pact with her:

Mom: [*Fifteen minutes before Leah comes over*] You can play with Barbies if you agree to let Leah be in charge of what you play. You have a choice: either let Leah be in charge of what you play, or we'll put the Barbies away until Leah leaves. What would you like to do?

Natalie: I'll let Leah pick what we do.

Mom: Good. We'll give it a try. If you can't let Leah choose, then you'll have to put the Barbies away. Okay?

Natalie: Okay.

Plan A: If Natalie insists on playing with Barbies when Leah is no longer interested:

Mom takes her Barbies away for the remainder of the play date. She also makes Barbies off limits for the next few play dates. This is how she makes the point that friends are more important than Barbies. Natalie should not bring Barbies to school or after-school care, since it is likely she is behaving the same way there.

Plan B: If Natalie lets Leah choose:

This is helping Natalie kick her addiction. Mom makes the same pact each time another girl comes over to play.

THE NEXT STEP:

Congratulations! You have helped your child cut down on activities that cut out friends. Now it's time to find activities that require playmates. In the next chapter you will learn how to help your child develop interests which attract friends.

3
DEVELOPING INTERESTS THAT ATTRACT FRIENDS

THE PROBLEM:

My child doesn't seem to want to play with other children. What can I do about this?

My child isn't a sports person. What should I do about it?

My daughter doesn't have the same interests as other girls. What should I do?

BACKGROUND: Cultivation of a child's interests

Mutual interests are the language of friendship. I have several acquaintances whom I like very much. When I think about getting together with them, I can't think of anything to do which we would both enjoy. That's why they're only acquaintances.

Solitary interests, such as reading, help make a well-rounded human being, but they don't help children find friends. This chapter shows you how to nurture interactive interests that lure friends. I'm talking about activity interests like board games, sports, doll play, and pretend games, which feed friendships. Children with friends have interests that make them want to play and talk with others.

The appeal of interactive interests

Alan, age eight, brought a Nerf football to the playground. The playground doesn't supply toys. None of the other boys there had thought to bring a toy. Without asking anyone to play, Alan immediately had two playmates. He isn't that good at football, just good enough so that he can enjoy a game of catch. The three boys tossed the ball around for an hour before they got tired.

As with all ice-breakers, it's not enough for Alan to have the toy. He must know how to use it, or the children will not like playing with him. The Nerf football helps the boys to get to know each other because the toy is easy to share. If the toy were a radio controlled car, other children would be attracted. Instead of harmonious play for an hour, you'd see minor squabbling for 15 minutes over whose turn it is.

Hannah began attending a dance class with two other nine-year-old girls she knew. She met another girl in the class who also went to her school. After a few months, the four girls started doing things together. The girls talk about this class endlessly. They also practice new routines together and trade clothes.

Studies show that girls slowly include others in their friendship circle. It takes a while for Hannah and her friends to form a friendship circle. They meet regularly at class. The common activity leads to common interests. Common interests give the girls something to talk about and a reason to get together.

You can help your child become interested in activities that attract others. If you've tried, and your child resists learning new games, here's how you can overcome this.

SOLVING THE PROBLEM:
Increase your child's interest in interactive toys

Some toys draw your child to play with others. But your child won't know how much fun they are until he starts to play with them.

Step 1: Help your child select good interactive toys.

Good interactive toys are fun to play only if they are played with someone else. Make sure your child has some interactive toys.

> *Jason is seven years old and has never gone over to another child's house, nor has he invited another child over to his house. He has plenty of books. He likes to draw, has art materials and lots of videotapes. He doesn't know how to play any games which the other children his age play. At school, while the other children are playing handball, Jason is playing in the sandbox by himself.*

If you have asked your child what toys he wants or taken him to toy stores and he doesn't want anything, you may think he lacks interest in toys. But, your child may not be able to make an informed choice. In Jason's case, it is up to his parents to generate the interest. They should start by getting one inside and one outside toy that has the important qualities listed below.

1. *Requires two persons (indoor toys) or at least two persons (outdoor toys) to play.*
   If your child likes to play it, then he will be hungry for playmates.

2. *Does not encourage aggression.*
   Water pistols seem harmless, but feelings get hurt when kids get soaked. Avoid toys with projectiles of any kind— arrows or ninja weapons.

3. *Is fun for you and your child to play.*
   You will teach him the game, so you might as well enjoy it.

4. *Has simple rules.*
   Your child will not need your help to play with a friend.
   Your child won't lose patience learning the game. You won't

lose patience teaching it. Your child can easily teach it to others who don't know how to play.

5. *Does not take too long for your child to play.*
   If he loses interest in games after an hour, get a game that usually ends before 45 minutes.

6. *Is inexpensive.*
   It will not be a great loss if it isn't played.

Balls and jump ropes are good outdoor toys. Foursquare, Wiffle, or Nerf balls are excellent because they are easy to hit, but can't be easily hit out of the play yard. Chinese and regular jump ropes, and hopscotch are portable. To get more ideas, watch (with your child) what other children are playing at school or a local playground.

Board games are good activities for your home. Starting in second grade, my son and his friends were able to play Parcheesi, checkers, Don't break the ice, Mr. Wiggly, and Chutes and ladders without adult help. They needed adult help with Clue Junior and Monopoly Junior until fourth grade, and could play Monopoly in fifth grade. Use the recommended ages on the game as a guide.

Step 2: Play with your child.

Children have to watch a game played or try to play it themselves in order to become interested. Play with your child to get him interested in these toys. Start out with a game that you like to play, so that you will have fun too. I find this is an especially important activity for dads who are, want to be, or need to be kids at heart. Studies show that the self-esteem of boys and girls is higher when their dads play with them regularly.

> *Mary, age seven, doesn't know the rules to any board games. When she plays with other girls, she has difficulty keeping up, since the rules are new to her. She frequently annoys the others by making up her own rules without their agreement. She argues over who is correct instead of having fun.*

Mary's dad should start with a game with a few simple rules and avoid playing games where she makes up the rules. Either of two things will happen next:

Plan A: If Mary obeys the rules of the simpler game:
Mary probably made up her own rules to the other games because she was embarrassed that she didn't know them. Mary's dad should teach her the rules of more games, but should go slowly.

Plan B: If Mary continues to make up rules:
Mary wants to be in charge. May's dad shouldn't let her make up rules as she goes along. He should discourage this behavior:

Mary: I get to go twice.
Dad: [*In a quiet, neutral tone of voice*] It's no fun to play unless you stick by the rules.
Mary: But I want to go twice.
Dad: We'll have to stop. I'll be glad to play with you some more when you can obey the rules.
Mary: Okay, you go next.
Dad: Thank you [*then slightly exaggerates that he is enjoying the game*].

Allow your child to negotiate rules. Negotiation means that the child gets others to agree before going on. Examples:

1. *Asking for extra practice:*
   Mary asks rather than insists she go again. Other kids can say no to this but most won't, so Dad allows this.

Mary: [*Throws the basketball and misses*] I wasn't ready. Can I go again?
Dad: Okay.

2. *Agreeing on the rules before the start of play:*

Shelby: [*Sets up Chinese jump rope*] Let's have Chanceys (going again if you miss), OK?
Dad: I tell you what. You can have chanceys and I won't, OK?
Shelby: OK.

Step 3: Make sure your child wins.
One reason why some children don't like interactive toys is that they get discouraged when they lose. You can rig the game so that

your child experiences winning during the time he ordinarily would be discouraged. Some people call this reverse cheating. I call it encouragement. Be subtle about it, so your child won't notice you're doing this. The goal is to encourage your child to feel confident and like the game, so that she will become hooked on it. You should continue to let her win until she notices it and insists you play to the level of your skill (by then she's hooked on the game). Then you're sunk if you're any good because she will get tired of playing with you and move on to others her age who are closer in skill. Wallow in your success! Don't worry. She'll come back to you to teach her some more games.

Step 4: Use Tactful Praise with your child.

Tactful Praise is the most powerful way you can improve your child's self-confidence. School-aged children are very sensitive and feel put down if praise isn't tactful. Here's how to Tactfully Praise 5 to 12-year-olds:

1. *Eye contact:*
   Look your child in the eye.

2. *Body language:*
   Make sure you are as close to your child as the situation will allow. Calling out a praising remark from the sidelines near your child is more effective than from the other side of the field. Leaning over towards your child during a board game is better than yelling.

3. *Voice tone:*
   Clearly audible and slightly warm (for children above seven) or very warm (for 5 to 7-year-olds). Louder from the sidelines. Too much warmth makes older children feel you're treating them like a baby.

4. *Content:*
   Make it short, but say exactly what your child did that you liked. Examples:
   "It was nice of you to let me go first."
   "That was a nice try."
   "Good move."

5. *Timing:*

   Praise is private, not distracting, and given as soon after the act as possible. Don't wait for the perfect behavior to praise. Start with 25 per cent of perfect.

   Good times to praise:

   Right after a clever or considerate move in a board game.

   Immediately after a good catch in a baseball game.

   On the way home from a team practice or class.

6. *Avoid discouraging statements:*

   Don't talk about your child's faults or what she can't do well in front of others.

   Don't label your child in a negative way: "He's not a sports person."

   Don't label your child by comparison: "He's more athletic than his brother."

   Don't spoil praise, for example: "That's good, now why couldn't you have done that before?", or "Next time I'm sure you'll do better." These are demoralizing statements.

You may see your child glow after Tactful Praise. Some children do, and others don't, but they are usually more willing to play with you the next time you ask. Or they may even ask you to play.

Use lots of Tactful Praise with your child for two reasons. First, Tactful Praise makes your child feel better about her own performance. Second, it's catching. When you praise your child for trying ("nice shot," "good try"), she will begin to use it with other children. Other children prefer to play with a child who praises rather than criticizes them.

THE NEXT STEP:

Congratulations! If you've followed the steps in this chapter, you've helped your child become a better playmate and raised your child's self-confidence. You've expanded your child's interest in activities that will be fun for her to share. Once your child has a couple of dependable activities, the children she plays with will expand her interests more. The next chapter helps you to help your child meet others who will want to be better friends.

4
FINDING FRIENDS IN YOUR NEIGHBORHOOD

THE PROBLEM:

My child is not meeting any children he likes. How can I help?

My child's friends live too far away to have play dates. What can I do?

I don't see any children out in my neighborhood, but I know there are some. How can I help my child find them?

BACKGROUND:
Social support for you and your child

Children make friends themselves; parents help make this possible by helping them find others to make friends with.

> *Sandy is a kind, 42-year-old single woman who adopted seven-year-old Barbara two years ago. Although both had some rocky times adjusting to each other, they get along quite well now. Sandy belongs to a socially active church and is friends with many of the single adults and childless couples of the congregation.*

On the other hand, she knows no other parents of seven-year-old girls. She drops her daughter off at Brownie meetings, but doesn't have time to talk to the other parents. Although well-behaved and liked by other children at school, her daughter has no close friends and is often lonely for a playmate.

Barbara changed Sandy's life in many important ways but Sandy's social supports failed to support Barbara's needs. I recommended to Sandy that she meet the other parents of girls in Barbara's class. As Sandy began to meet these parents, she arranged play dates and Barbara began to develop closer friends. Think about your family, friends and acquaintances—how do they give you support? There are two different categories:

1. *Emotional support.*
   Some adults talk with you about things that are bothering you. You turn to them about life decisions and conflicts with other adults. These are your closest friends and family.

2. *Helpful support.*
   Parents you share car pools or trade babysitting with are good examples.

When you think about your helpful support, notice that the people close by, either in your neighborhood or at work, help you more often.

SOLVING THE PROBLEM:
Finding friends in your neighborhood

The steps in this chapter help the child who has adequate free time and would like to use it to find others to play with. The child who is already in many activities may need to cut back (see Chapter 1).

Step 1: Enroll your child at your neighborhood school.

Sending your child to a neighborhood school has the following social advantages:

1. Your child will meet children who live nearby. It will be easier for you to hang around at school and meet other parents, which is one of the most productive ways of helping your child find friends. Children are invisible in many neighborhoods (they usually are indoors or in their backyard). They become visible at the neighborhood school.

2. Children don't have far to go for play dates. Children plan their own play dates better when they get older, since transportation is less of a problem.

What I mean by a neighborhood school is one within a ten minute drive of your home. It need not be a public school.

> *Nine year-olds Anthony and Howard have become best of friends. They have attended the same school together since kindergarten. They've been in the same classrooms for two years. Their parents can easily arrange play dates, since they frequently meet on the school grounds and talk to each other. Both boys live within walking distance of the school and each other. They frequently call each other to find out about homework. Both mothers are on the school PTA and frequently work together on school fund-raisers.*

Many parents do not send their child to the neighborhood school because they are uncomfortable with its academic or social atmosphere. These are very important factors to consider. But success in life is influenced by a combination of academic achievement and "EQ" or social skill. Whether or not your child attends a school in your neighborhood, it's important for you to use your neighborhood resources to find children with whom your child can easily play. You might even find a parent you want to be friends with. The next steps help you to do this.

Step 2: Look for neighborhood activities.
Look for one activity to join in your neighborhood. Never involve your child in more than two activities at a time, because you won't have enough time for one-on-one play dates. There are three varieties of neighborhood activities to consider: classes (dance,

ballet, karate, science), groups (scouts, theater, day camps) and team sports. Studies show that activities for "girls only" enhance a girl's self-esteem better than coed activities. I feel this is because supervisors of most coed activities pay less attention to girls than boys. On the other hand, coed activities can teach both boys and girls how to get along with each other better. Organized activities all share the following possible benefits:

◆ They offer opportunities to meet other children and parents and a place to see them frequently.

◆ They provide topics of conversation and shared interests.

Team sports may provide the following additional benefits for your child:

◆ Learning how to work better in a group.

◆ Learning how to lose gracefully.

You say you don't know of any neighborhood resources? Take a driving tour of your neighborhood with your child. After school one day or on the weekend are good times to do this.

1. Look for local parks which are safe and adequately maintained where children your child's age are playing. Go into the park office and check for after-school programs, team sports and vacation day camps. Many of these are seasonal—teams correspond to their season of professional play. Sign-up is usually one to two months before the start of the season.

2. Look for public or private schools. Your neighborhood school yard may have after-school play programs open to your child, even if he doesn't attend that school.

3. Call the scouting district office. They will put you in touch with leaders of units in your area. My Cub Scout pack reorganizes every September. If a parent calls me then, I will be organizing entire new dens. If parents call me later in the year, I will check to see if any den leaders can take more children.

Step 3: Investigate by asking questions.

Call the contact person and ask questions about the activity you are thinking of having your child join. Telephone manners tell you a lot. Good questions to ask (in addition to date and time of events):

1. Do you have groups for children my child's age and sex?

2. Are other children from my area or my child's school attending?

3. Will I be asked to be involved in any way?

4. Can I have names of past participants and current leaders?

The contact person may not be able to give you all the information you'd like, but may be able to refer you to someone who can. The more you learn, the easier for you to determine if the activity is a good fit for your child and your family.

THE NEXT STEP:

You've found good neighborhood resources. Convenience is only one of many advantages of these resources. You and your child can make easily maintained and enduring friendships. Chapter 5 will show you how to use the resources you've found so that you and your child will get the most benefit.

5
USING ORGANIZED ACTIVITIES TO FIND FRIENDS

THE PROBLEM:

How can I help my child find friends through neighborhood activities?

BACKGROUND:
Organized activities and your child's friendships

The most common suggestion parents give each other to help their child make friends is to put them in an organized activity. Usually it's a team, class or scouts. This is a good suggestion, but parents don't realize it is only the first step. Research shows that organized activities don't improve friendships by themselves. I'll show you how to insure that friendships do develop outside the activity.

SOLVING THE PROBLEM:
Joining neighborhood organized activities

So you found an activity that looks good to you. What do you do next?

Step 1: Make the first two visits mandatory, then let your child choose to continue.

Your first priority is to get your child to give it a try. Make it mandatory that she go at least twice, so that she can make an informed choice. Nine-year-old Melissa resists new activities, but has some athletic ability:

Mom: How about taking gymnastics?

Melissa: No. It's boring, and I won't know anyone there.

Mom: Have you ever seen the class?

Melissa: No, but I don't think I'd like it.

Mom: There's a class this Saturday. I want you to try it for at least two times.

Melissa: Do I have to?

Mom: Yes. If you don't like it after the second time, then we can stop if you want.

If you can't get your child to try new activities, read Chapter 22.

Step 2: The first time in any activity, make sure your child follows four basic rules.

It's important for your child to make a good first impression. She will not make friends if she doesn't follow these basic rules of etiquette:

1. *Take the activity seriously*; don't clown around. Children should be quiet and attentive to the adult. Making faces or silly sounds or whispering is annoying to everyone.

2. *Don't try to make friends or talk to other children while you're supposed to be paying attention to the adult.*

3. *Stay in your own assigned area*; don't interfere with someone else's performance. Giving other children instructions in classes, or running all over the field to make catches are clear violations of this rule.

4. *Don't criticize others.* Either praise others or be quiet.

Ask yourself if your child can follow these four basic rules. If the answer is yes, go on to step 3. If not, review these four rules with your child immediately before you try out the new activity:

Dad: I'm glad you're going to give Little League a try. I think you'll have fun. I want you to show everyone how nice you are. I want you to notice how the other kids are taking Little League seriously and that no one is clowning around. The coach will tell you where to play and that's where you have to stay.

Andrew: I know that.

Dad: Good. If anyone doesn't listen to the coach and plays in your position, tell me after practice, Okay?

Andrew: Okay.

Dad: If you see someone you want to make friends with, let's try to talk to them after practice, or maybe before the next practice, okay?

Andrew: Okay.

Notice how Dad left out rule #4 (Don't criticize). There's no good way to introduce this rule to your child before it happens. It works better to look for times when he breaks this rule and tell him about it then. You should supervise from the sidelines if you're not sure of your child.

Plan A: If your child follows these rules:

Praise your child on the way home (see Tactful Praise in Chapter 3). Consider yourself lucky and move on to Step 3.

Plan B: If your child violates one or more of the four basic rules:

Immediately after your child has broken a rule, pull him aside and quietly tell him the rule. Secure a promise from him to obey the rule. Example:

Dad: [*Observes Andrew getting into an argument with another boy. He immediately walks over*] Andrew, I need to speak to you for a moment. Come here, please.

Andrew: [*Keeps arguing.*]

Dad: [*Getting between Andrew and the other child*] I need to speak to you. Come with me. [*Takes Andrew off to the side*] You need to be quiet and watch home plate while you're in the outfield.

Andrew: But he was bothering me.

Dad: Then you need to stand far enough away from him so he won't bother you. Can you do that?

Andrew: OK.

Dad: Thanks.

If Andrew obeys his dad then he can continue with practice. Dad should use Tactful Praise (see Chapter 3) with Andrew after practice. Dad should continue to supervise Andrew until he is sure Andrew follows the four basic rules.

Plan C: If your child continues to break the four basic rules:
It's time to pull your child out of this activity. It doesn't do Andrew any good to continue with this activity if he can't behave appropriately. Andrew's dad needs to help him learn the Rules of a Good Sport (Chapters 6 and 7). In the meantime Andrew should avoid the following types of activities:

1. Activities which involve a lot of waiting, such as baseball.

2. Competitive activities, which bring out the worst in some children.

3. Combative activities such as karate are difficult for children who have trouble confining kicking and hitting to practice.

Step 3: Evaluate the adult supervisor.

Your next priority is to insure that your child will have a satisfactory experience that will build self-confidence rather than damage it. The benefits your child gets from sports and classes will depend on the adult supervisors. Most sports programs and public parks depend upon volunteer coaches. Professionals generally run martial arts classes for kids. Some of them are looking to make a name for their school, and put the welfare of the children second. Look for the qualities listed in the next table.

You won't find a perfect adult supervisor. I give most coaches and teachers high marks. I have rarely seen a poor coach working with first through third graders. In contrast, many coaches who

Qualities of adult supervisors

Good Supervisor	Poor Supervisor
Tries to teach children elements of playing/performing without expecting too much.	Trying your best isn't good enough; demands perfection.
Praises children for personal best or just trying.	Yells at children for not doing better. Argues with the game officials.
Works children at practice with a plan for improvement.	Has no plan, holds poorly thought-out practices with little or no instruction
Lets all of the children have fun.	Plays favorites while others warm the benches and receive no instruction.
Teaches consideration for others.	Teaches physical roughness for the purpose of winning. "Make sure you run over the second baseman."

work with children, age ten and older, focus upon winning and overlook sportsmanship to varying degrees. I understand their focus on winning: older children begin to see the team as a job in which others are counting on them. They are demoralized when they play on a team with children who can't play as well as everyone else. In my opinion, this doesn't justify poor sportsmanship.

What do you do if your child is on a team with a coach who shows many of the qualities of a poor supervisor? Two alternatives are:

1. Switch your child to another team. This will be hard to do, but always worth a try.

2. Drop your child from the team. You shouldn't be investing your precious time in an activity that will frustrate you and your child. Avoid a demoralizing experience.

Step 4: Cautiously involve yourself in the activity.

Next get to know other parents while your child is getting to know the other children. Hang out where the other parents are and socialize with them. If other parents watch the activity, then so should you. If there are several parents helping as assistants, offering to help may be a good opportunity to get to know them. However, if your child has social problems, I strongly advise against being the coach-parent.

◆ If you're like most parents, the competition will get some juices flowing in you which will interfere with your child's social growth.

◆ A coach may be more negative with his own child than with others on the team.

◆ Other children on the team may resent a child who gets preferential treatment by his coach-parent.

◆ The child of the coach may be more sassy than if his parent was not the coach.

Step 5: Make play dates with children your child likes.

This is the step that gives your child the more lasting social benefits of your work. You've met other parents and your child has met other children. Your child has made a good first impression. Now you can make arrangements to get the children together. You should always start this process by asking your child in private if he would like to play with someone. Example:

Dad: Is there anyone on your Little League team you would like to invite over for a couple of hours?

Andrew: I don't know.

Dad: How about Tommy? You seem to get along with him and I can ask his dad.

Andrew: Okay.

Start with a short play date before or after practice. See Chapters 9 and 10 for how to do this. I have summarized what you need to know to join activities in the checklist on the next page.

THE NEXT STEP:

You and your child have taken best advantage of that organized activity. Your child doesn't have to be talented in an activity to use it to meet friends. He needs only to know enough about it to have a good time and choose others to play with who are at the same skill level. You used that activity to help your child meet friends and to help you network with other parents. I remember how awkward I felt when I started to network. It got easier with practice and I made a good friend in the process.

Many children can take it from here, but some will need to know how to make friends on their own. Chapter 6 will show you how to help your child with this skill.

✔	Checklist for Joining Neighborhood Organized Activities
Step 1:	Make the first two visits mandatory, then let your child choose to continue.
Step 2:	The first time in any activity, have your child follow four basic rules: 1. Take the activity seriously; don't clown around. 2. Don't try to make friends or talk to other children while you're supposed to be paying attention to the adult (this is annoying to everybody). 3. Stay in your own assigned area; don't interfere with someone else's performance in a game or class. 4. Either praise others or be quiet; don't criticize others. Plan A: If your child follows these rules: Go to Step 3. Plan B: If your child violates these rules: Pull him aside immediately and quietly tell him the rule. If he obeys the rule, use Tactful Praise (p.28) Plan C: If your child continues to break the four basic rules: Teach him the Rules of a Good Sport (Chapter 7)
Step 3:	Evaluate the adult supervisor. If you have a poor supervisor, switch to another activity or drop the current one.
Step 4:	Cautiously involve yourself in the activity. Get to know the other parents. Make play dates for your child. Avoid being the coach-parent if your child has social problems.
Step 5:	Make play dates with children your child picks. (See Chapters 9 and 10 for how to do this.)

PART II: MAKING FRIENDS

A good friend is someone who is considerate of your child's feelings, someone whom she can trust to confide in. To have a good friend, your child must be a good friend. You can help teach your child how.

6
JOINING OTHERS AT PLAY

THE PROBLEM:

My child is uncomfortable meeting other children. How do I help?
My child can meet other children but soon alienates them. Can I help?

BACKGROUND: Making a good first impression

You will almost never see a child meet new children by introducing himself and shaking hands. Children make new acquaintances by joining others who are playing. Some children don't know how to do this and avoid it. Other children join in but do it in a way that quickly alienates others. This chapter will show you how to help your child meet new friends and make good first impressions in public. This is one of the most important social skills for children.

The rules of etiquette for joining others

Try this at the next party you attend—stand next to two people talking to each other. Look at them and say nothing, just listen. If they are talking about something interesting, stick around. If not, move on. Notice you don't hurt anyone's feelings if you move on.

If you're still hanging around, notice whether the people conversing start looking at you while they're talking. If they do, they have invited you into their conversation. If they don't look at you, they want to be alone. Notice again that you don't hurt anyone's feelings when you walk away. Rules of etiquette protect everyone's feelings.

Studies show that children use three approaches when near other children at play. Some children follow five rules of etiquette and easily join others. Some children break these rules. They may join others but quickly alienate them. Still other children don't know these rules, don't try to join others and wind up playing by themselves. How children join is shown in the next table.

How children join others at play

Follows Rules of Etiquette	Doesn't Know Rules —Doesn't Join	Breaks Rules of Etiquette
1. Watches the other children playing to show that he is interested. Figures out the game rules and who is winning. Checks that the skill level of the children playing is about the same as his.	Off by himself— doesn't watch others or watches from too far away.	Starts playing without knowing the game. -or- Attempts to disrupt the game. -or- Annoys children by asking what they are playing.
2. Watches silently or says something nice about children playing - "Nice shot,...nice try."	Doesn't watch closely enough.	Criticizes the children playing— "You stupid jerk, don't you know how to play?"
3. Waits for a pause in the game before asking to join.	Waits to be asked, never asks to join.	Barges in and begins playing.
4. BOYS: Asks to join the side that needs the most help (the losing side or side with fewer players). GIRLS: Asks the girl who owns the rope or ball to join.	Never asks to join.	BOYS: Joins the winning side, if he knows which side that is. GIRLS: Tries to make the others let her in— "If you don't let me play I'll tell the teacher."
5. Accepts no for an answer if not allowed to join.		Complains if told he can't join.

During one of my interviews with children, a well-liked seven-year-old girl surprised me by reciting all of the five rules in the left-hand column of the table without any help. In my interviews with girls and their mothers, I learned two other rules which girls have to follow to join other girls at play:

1. If you know a girl playing in a game you would like to join, you must first look to her. If she looks back at you, then you ask her if you may join the game.

2. If she doesn't look at you, she is letting you know you can't join.

Where and when

Many parents think it's okay for their child to try to meet others anywhere and anytime. I have found that it is better to encourage your child to try to make friends only at certain times and places. Studies show that children who try to make friends when the teacher or coach is talking, or when other children are trying to work in the classroom, do not make friends. Potential playmates reject these advances, not only because they might get in trouble, but they are usually annoyed when someone distracts them from their activity. Better times and places to try to make friends are:

◆ when children are waiting or unoccupied, for instance, before or after school, or before or after team practice.

◆ at playgrounds and lunchrooms.

I've found the steps in the next section to be effective for boys and girls who are in first grade or older (below first grade, children do not organize themselves in games). Boys will want to join other boys playing, while girls are successful at joining either girls or boys playing. If your child masters all the steps, then she will have skills to make her successful in joining others at play in any situation.

SOLVING THE PROBLEM: Joining children in play

Familiarize yourself with the five rules of etiquette in the left hand column of the table above and how to tell when they are broken. Coach your child about how to meet other children and make good first impressions. It will take more than one session for younger children to use these rules effectively. Your child will make errors and he will do some things well. This is inevitable. You are watching for improvement from session to session. I find that children are very interested in learning these rules. Remember, you are to teach and support your child, not do it for her.

Step 1: Search your neighborhood for a suitable public place.

Find a place in your neighborhood where several groups of children the same age or a little younger than your child play. A local playground or a school yard in your neighborhood, where children gather and organize their own games are the best bets. Pick a safe place where you are comfortable with the children who are playing. Do this at least a day before you try Step 2.

Step 2: Watch a group of children at play.

Bring a newspaper or magazine along with you. Have your child pick a group of children at play. Pick children who appear to be the same age or slightly younger and about the same skill level or slightly less skilled than your child.

Do pick children who are about as skilled as your child at the game they are playing.

Don't pick older children as they are less likely to accept your child as an equal.

Don't pick children your child already knows.

Don't criticize your child in any way as he tries to join.

You and your child should begin by watching a game in play from about 20-30 feet away. Watching a game from the sidelines is the way your child gets information and lets the other children know he wants to play. It's a no risk way to join, because sometimes the children playing will ask onlookers to join.

You need to be alongside your child in this step to make sure he gets the most benefit. Don't be disappointed if your child isn't asked to play. It's important for him to learn the basics first.

Children having a good time playing are usually annoyed by being asked what they are playing. They are also irritated by children who join a game but don't know what's going on. Have your child whisper to you what the children are playing, what the rules are, if there are teams, who is winning, (for girls, ask if she knows who brought the toy the children are playing with) and any other details of the game that are important. Here's how a dad coaches his son, Keith:

Dad:	[*Pointing to five children at play in the distance*] Do you want to play with those kids?
Keith:	I don't know.
Dad:	Let's stay here and watch what they're doing. Let's look at those kids first. See if you can tell me what they're playing and what the rules are. [*They watch for five minutes and Keith correctly answers what game it is, who is on which team, who is winning.*] That's great. You understand what's happening. Which side would need your help the most?
Keith:	The side with only two kids on it. The other side has three.
Dad:	That's right!

This is a very important question. Your child needs to be looking to join the side that needs the most help, *not* the side that's winning. The children playing will welcome this kind of help, since it evens up the game and makes it more fun for all.

Step 3: Help your child think of how to join in.

Dad will help Keith think of how to join the game by focusing on two things Keith needs to know—when to join and what to say. A pause in the game or the end of a round are ideal times to ask to join. They do not interrupt the flow of the game and show the children at play that Keith is considerate and knowledgeable.

Dad:	Which side will you ask to join?
Keith:	The side with only two on it.
Dad:	That's right. What can you ask them?

Keith: Do you need another guy on your team?

Dad: That sounds great. When would be a good time to ask?

Keith: After someone scores a basket.

Dad: That might work!

For girls, you should add:

Mom: Whose ball is it?

Laura: It's that girl's [*pointing*].

Mom: That's right. So who would you ask if you wanted to play?

Laura: The girl whose ball it is.

Mom: Great!

Step 4: Review with your child why children are kept out of a game.

Being turned down from games is a fact of life. The table below lists reasons I commonly find for children being turned down, and what to do about it:

Getting turned down

Reasons for being turned down	What to do about it
Something you did to them before (avoided them, gotten them in trouble with the teacher, etc.).	Treat others as you would have them treat you. Choose another group to join.
Tried to join in the wrong way.	Next time, watch first and praise other kids. Wait for a pause in the action to ask to join.
They are too popular, too athletic, not interested in the same things you are.	Pick other children closer in skill and interests.
They don't want to meet new friends.	Pick other children.
They misunderstood what you wanted to do.	Say it differently, e.g., point out that they have two less kids on their side.
They didn't feel like playing with you just then.	Try again later.

Bottom Line: Take "No!" for an answer and move on.

Children without friendship problems are turned down frequently and are not concerned by it. Your child should expect to be turned down about half the time he attempts to join others. Far from being a crushing event, being turned down should get your child to look for another group of children playing. You should prepare your child for this *before* he attempts to join in. You do this by speaking about "another child." A sample conversation:

Dad: Why might those kids not want another boy to play?
Keith: I don't know.
Dad: Suppose the boy was mean to them before?
Keith: Then they probably wouldn't like him and wouldn't let him play.
Dad: Yeah. What other reasons might they have?
Keith: Maybe they just didn't like him.
Dad: Maybe they knew he played much better than they did.
Keith: Yeah.
Dad: Maybe they didn't want to meet anyone new.
Keith: Yeah.
Dad: What's the best thing you could do if some boys don't want to play with you just when you want to?
Keith: I don't know.
Dad: Which one sounds good to you: Try other kids or try again later? [*They're both good alternatives.*]
Keith: Try other kids.
Dad: That's a good choice. Who else will you try if the kids we are watching don't want you to join in?
Keith: [*Pointing*] Those kids playing handball.
Dad: Yes!

Dad is encouraging Keith to solve this for himself, but when he doesn't know, Dad gives him a choice of two alternatives. This keeps Keith involved in the process of discovery.

Step 5: Coach your child to praise other children's behavior.

You are teaching your child how to tactfully let others at play know that he is interested in joining. One powerful way to do this is for him to praise the children. Children who receive praise themselves are more apt to praise others. If you have started using Tactful Praise (Chapter 3), and if you praise your child for trying his best now, it is more likely that he will praise others. Praise is contagious.

Examples of praise your child can use for the children he is watching are "nice try," (for a near-basket) or "great shot," (for a basket).

Dad: [*Waiting until a child playing almost gets a basket*] What is something nice you can say about that shot?

Keith: I don't know.

Dad: How about "nice try!" Tell me when you can say something nice about what one of the kids in the game does.

Keith: [*Another child makes a good shot and Keith says nothing.*]

Dad: How about that shot?

Keith: Oh yeah, [*calls out*] nice shot.

Dad: Right!

This is hard for some children to do. Go on to Step 6 even if your child doesn't get it.

Step 6: Encourage your child to try to join.

The other way your child tactfully shows his interest in joining is to move to within ten feet of the group at play. Getting this close sends the message to the children at play that your child is interested in this game. Encourage your child to join after your child tells you when and who he will ask to play. You move back to a bench to read your newspaper.

Dad: See if the kids will let you play. Go ahead and get closer to them. Stand over there and watch them

> [*pointing to the sidelines of the game*]. I'll be sitting over at that bench over there [*pointing*].

Keith: Okay. [*Dad now backs away about ten more feet, sits on a nearby bench and pretends to read a newspaper or magazine, while actually watching.*]

Plan A: If your child was successful at joining:

You want to have your child end his participation on a good note. If your child generally gets along well with children, then allow your child to play until the game ends. If your child frequently gets into arguments with children, allow your child to play only for about ten minutes. He needs to learn the Rules of a Good Sport in the next chapter, and is not yet ready to play on his own. Here's how Mom tactfully pulls Laura out of the game:

Mom: [*Walking up close to where Laura joined some other girls at play*] I'm sorry Laura. We're going to have to leave soon. I need to do some errands.

Laura: Oh Mom, I just started playing!

Mom: I'm sorry. You can play with these girls again the next time we're here.

Laura: Can I finish my next turn?

Mom: That's okay with me. Is it okay with the girls?

Plan B: If your child wasn't successful at joining:

Review the reasons for rejection (Step 4). Have your child pick the reason why she wasn't allowed to join just now. Here's an example in which a group of girls did not let Laura join:

Mom: How did it go?

Laura: They said no when I asked if I could play.

Mom: Well I'm glad you listened to them and went away. Why don't you think they wanted you to play?

Laura: They were being mean.

Mom: Well maybe they were, but let's see if you followed all the rules. Do you know which girl brought the ball?

Laura: The tall girl with blond hair.

Mom: Good! Who did you ask to join?

Laura: I asked the girl with red hair.

Mom: Oh. Well, who should you have asked?

Laura: I guess, I should have asked the tall blond girl.

Laura's mom should now have Laura repeat Steps 1-6 with another group of children.

Step 7: Praise your child.

Privately praise your child for attempts to follow your advice, *whether or not the attempts were successful.*

Plan A: If your child was successful:

Here's an example in which Keith has just finished playing well with a group of children he has joined:

Dad: [*Still pretending to read a magazine when Keith comes up to him. Quietly, he says*] You did a good job—it worked that time! I liked how you looked interested in the game the kids were playing before you asked to join.

Plan B: If your child was not successful:

In this example, Keith watched kids playing and asked to join them but they ignored him.

Dad: [*Still pretending to read a magazine, when Keith comes up to him*]. Well, you did everything you needed to do—you watched, then waited for a good time. I liked how you were able to take no for an answer. What could you do next?

Keith: Try other kids?

Dad: That's right! Let's see who else looks interesting to play with [*starts the process over again*].

I have summarized the steps to teach your child in the checklist on the next page.

THE NEXT STEP:

Your child now has a much better chance of meeting others and making a good first impression, even when you're not around! If your child plays well with others, repeat these steps several times to get your child comfortable with her new skill. She might be able to get telephone numbers from those other children (you'll use them to help your child start making close friends in Chapter 9). If your child has difficulty being considerate in group games and quickly alienates others, then go on to the next chapter to teach her the Rules of a Good Sport.

✔	Checklist for Joining Other Children at Play
Step 1:	Search your neighborhood for a suitable public place to meet other children.
Step 2:	Watch a group of children at play. Bring a magazine or newspaper to pretend to read at the appropriate time. Begin by watching a game from 20-30 feet away: Pick children the same age or slightly younger and at about the same skill level as your child. Does your child know the rules? Does your child know who is winning or who needs the most help? (Girls only) Does she know which girl brought the toy?
Step 3:	Coach your child about how to join. Your child should wait for a break in the activity before attempting to join. Your child should attempt to join the team that needs the most help. Have your child rehearse what she will say to try to join.
Step 4:	Review with your child why children are kept out of a game. Bottom line: take no for an answer and move on to other children playing.
Step 5:	Coach your child to praise other children's behavior.
Step 6:	Encourage your child to attempt to join. Your child moves to within ten feet, you move back to a bench. Watch from afar, pretending to read the newspaper/magazine you brought. Plan A: If your child was successful at joining—end on a good note Wait until the end of the game (if your child generally plays well with others) -or- Wait ten minutes and take your child out of the game (if your child has trouble playing with others) Plan B: If your child was not successful at joining—try again Review the reasons for rejection - which was it just now? Try Steps 1-6 again with another group of children.
Step 7:	Praise your child for the things she did well.

7
BECOMING
A GOOD
SPORT

THE PROBLEM:
How can I get my child to argue and brag less during games?

BACKGROUND: Keeping others as playmates
Once a year, my Cub Scout pack has its annual Pinewood Derby. The Cubs race cars that they and their dads build. Everyone gets a prize—participation, best design, most unusual... —only one wins the derby.

My first year as Cubmaster, I was particularly struck by several cubs who cried when they lost. They were supposed to be having fun! I decided that the reason they were feeling miserable was that no one told them to have fun, rather than to try to win.

The next year, I started off the event by telling them they were there to have fun and to show that they could be a good sport. Only one Cub would win. No one cried this time. Being a good sport was as important as winning to those kids.

The last chapter helped you teach your child how to start playing with others without one strike against him because of the way he entered the game. If he constantly squabbles with other children then he probably is playing to win at all costs and he isn't thinking about keeping others as playmates. The following table lists the ways a good sport plays differently from the child who plays to win at all costs.

How winning at all costs differs from being a good sport

Good Sport	Win at all costs
1. Takes the game seriously.	Clowns around—e.g., steals the ball and doesn't give it back.
2. Follows the rules of the game.	Frequently breaks the rules.
3. Lets other children have a good time by staying in position and waiting turn. Example: He plays only first base.	Tries to play all positions, doesn't let others play. Example: He makes diving catches all over the infield, doesn't let others have a turn.
4. Avoids arguments.	Gets angry and gets into arguments by playing referee. Example: "That was a foul, you're out"
5. Stays until the end of the game.	Walks away when tired of playing or losing.

You saw in the last chapter how joining others at play is a skill which children can and like to learn. I find it's the same with being a good sport. Children who don't follow rules of etiquette usually don't know them. You may be surprised, as I was, that the child who plays to win at all costs is glad when someone teaches him this valuable lesson in life.

SOLVING THE PROBLEM:
Teaching good sportsmanship

Return to the park or playground where you successfully practiced last chapter's steps. This time you will have at least three Good Sport Sessions to teach your child additional rules of etiquette, The Rules of a Good Sport.

If your child sees some of the children he was successful joining last time, he can approach them again. You stopped them from playing last time in order to leave on a good note. Now comes the payoff for doing this. Begin by following the first six steps below.

Step 1: Bring an ice breaker toy and a magazine for you to pretend to read.

Your child should still try the techniques learned in the last chapter to join others at play. Even if children aren't already playing when you arrive at your playground or park, your child should be ready to start playing anyway by bringing an icebreaker toy.

Wanda, age eight, brought a Chinese jump rope to school. When two other girls saw what she had, they immediately wanted to play with her. Since it was her rope, she could make the rules simple enough so that she could have a good time. They all had a good time for the entire 20 minutes of recess.

Bringing a toy to public places can break the ice. The outside toys you picked in Chapter 3 are ideal for this:

Do bring a ball, jump rope, or chalk (for hopscotch).

Don't bring one at a time activities like videogames, drawing materials, radio-controlled cars, or books.

Don't bring violent activities like ninja weapons, toy guns, water pistols or any toy that shoots projectiles.

Also bring a newspaper or magazine for you to pretend to read.

Step 2: Teach the Rules of a Good Sport.

Teach the your child the Rules of a Good Sport. It will be impossible for your child to abide by these rules and try to win at all costs. Problems playing with others will disappear. I list the rules in the best order to teach them, and then I'll show you how:

1. *Take the game seriously—no clowning around.*
   A child who clowns around when others are taking a game seriously makes a poor first impression.

2. *No refereeing.*
   Refereeing means pointing out rule violations ("You got there after I tagged you"), or criticizing others ("That was a stupid thing to do").

3. *Let others have fun too.*
   Even if your child is better than the other players at a particular sport, the idea is for everyone to have fun. Your child should stay in her own area and wait her turn, not try to catch any balls that someone else could catch or take too long for her turn.

4. *Praise other children.*
   Examples are "great shot" and "nice try," and giving the high-five to members of one's team.

5. *If bored, suggest a change in activity or switching positions.* Examples:

   > *Keith:* [*After getting tired of catching balls batted to him by Daniel.*] How about if I hit the ball and you catch for a while? [-or-]

   > *Keith:* Could we play for just five minutes more? I'm getting tired.

6. *Suggest a new rule instead of arguing.*
   Don't say: "That was a foul. You're out"
   Do say: "Let's make a rule that the foul line (pointing) is a take-over, OK?"
   Keith accepts either a yes or no answer and abides by it.

7. *If you win, pretend that winning wasn't important to you.*

8. *Do not walk away from a game when you are losing or tired of playing.*

Make sure your child knows the first two (younger children) or first four (older children) Rules of a Good Sport before beginning to play. Talk to your child while you are on your way to the Good Sport Session. Make sure there are no distractions, such as your car radio. Briefly review the rules:

Dad: We're heading for the same park where we met those kids last time. I want you to remember four rules of a good sport: Let other kids play their own positions, no clowning around, let someone else be the referee, and try to say a nice things to the other kids. Okay?

Keith: Okay.

Dad: What were the four rules?

Keith: Let other kids play their own positions, don't clown around, let someone else referee and what else?

Dad: Try saying things like "good shot," or "nice try," like you did last time, okay?

Keith: Okay.

Step 3: Encourage your child to attempt to join.

Your child should repeat the joining steps from the last chapter until she is accepted into a group so that you can do your Good Sport coaching. She should stand on the sidelines, within 10 feet, watching others in play. If she has brought a toy, she gives it to you to hold. You watch from 20 to 30 feet away. If your child is turned down, then she should try to join other children or she should start playing with the toy that she brought. If another child approaches while she's playing with the toy, she should ask her to play.

Step 4: See that your child follows the Rules of a Good Sport.

Continue to watch from afar. Relax and pretend to read that magazine. You're not *really* reading but watching your child. You are looking for:

- ♦ your child to follow the Rules of a Good Sport. You will be praising her for this in private after the game.

- ♦ your child breaking a Good Sport Rule you've taught her.

- ♦ instances where you have to teach her rules 5-8.

Plan A: If your child occasionally breaks a Good Sport Rule you have taught him:

Old habits die hard. It's only natural that your child will break a Good Sport Rule. Take her aside immediately and *quietly remind her in a neutral tone of voice* of the broken rule. Although reminding your child in this way disrupts the game and may frustrate the other children, I have found that they continue playing and ignore what's going on. They're more interested in the game than what's happening to your child. Remember, your goal here is to instruct your child so she can return to play and successfully apply the rule. Example:

Mom: [*Walking up to Laura*] Laura, I need to speak to you for a moment.

Laura: I'm playing right now.

Mom: Come over here for a minute, please.

Laura: [*Comes, with complaining voice*] What, Mom?

Mom: [*Whispering*] Thanks for coming over. Remember the rules of a good sport?

Laura: Yeah.

Mom: What are they?

Laura: Let other kids play their own positions, and I don't remember the rest.

Mom: Take the game seriously, let someone else be the referee, and try to say a couple of nice things to the others.

Laura: Oh yeah.

Mom: You need to let someone else be the referee. Let someone else point out when someone trips on the jump rope. Can you do that?

Laura: Yes, Mom.

Mom: Okay, you can go back to play now.

At first Laura will need several reminders like this. But after several Good Sport Sessions, following the rules becomes a habit.

Plan B: Your child breaks a rule you haven't told him yet:
Introduce new rules as instances come up. For instance, when you see your child having an argument, immediately take your child aside. In a neutral tone, whisper the sixth rule of a good sport:

Dad: [*Taking Keith over to one side after the beginning of an argument over where the foul line is*] I want to tell you about another rule of a good sport—instead of arguing, suggest a new rule.

Keith: But he hit the ball out of bounds!

Dad: Just ask him if you can have a new rule. Say "How about we make that the foul line?" If he doesn't want to, then you will have to accept where he says the foul line is. Can you do that?

Keith: Why do I have to?

Dad: You need to be a good sport.

Keith: Okay.

Dad: Thanks. Now you can go back and play.

Step 5: Don't let your child end the game unless his playmates agree.

Your child should not walk away from a game when he is losing or tired of playing. He needs to be considerate of everyone's feelings. The other children are counting on your child to help them play the game. This is how it's done:

Keith: [*Leaving game while others still want to play*] I don't want to play anymore.

Dad: [*Walking to Keith from his bench*] Keith, ask the other boys and see if they want to stop.

Keith: But I'm tired of playing.

Dad: You still need to check with them. What do you ask them?

Keith: Is it okay if we stop?

Step 6: Praise your child.

If your child was able to follow any Rule of a Good Sport, praise your child about it in private after the game. Example:

Dad: [*On the way home from the park*] I liked the way you took the game seriously.

If your child had trouble following the rules, proceed to Step 7.

Step 7: Make a pact with your child before the next Good Sport Session.

Immediately before a Good Sport Session Make a deal with your child. Offer a small reward that you can give easily and immediately after the session. If the rules were broken seven times in the previous Good Sport session, offer a reward for three or less infractions this time. Example:

> *Dad:* Before you play with those children, remember the four rules of a good sport?
>
> *Keith:* What rules?
>
> *Dad:* Let other kids play their own positions, take the game seriously, let someone else be the referee, and try to say a couple of nice things to the others.
>
> *Keith:* Okay.
>
> *Dad:* It's been hard for you to remember them. How about a special treat if you remember today?
>
> *Keith:* Could we go for ice cream?
>
> *Dad:* It's a deal. If I don't remind you more than three times about the rules then we will go for ice cream.

Dad should remove Keith from the activity after each time Keith forgets a Good Sport Rule and let him return after he has promised to follow the rule. If Dad has to remind Keith three or fewer times, Keith gets the ice cream. If you have made a pact with your child, don't count the first time Rules 5-8 are broken. If Keith has to be reminded more than three times, then Dad tells him that next time he can try again, but this time they skip the ice cream.

Next time Dad makes the play time shorter (Dad should reduce it from 1/2 hour to 20 minutes) and makes the same pact with Keith. He should take Keith out for ice cream if there are three or fewer infractions.

The table on the next page summarizes all of the steps of the Good Sport Session.

THE NEXT STEP:

Repeat the Good Sport Sessions until your child is able to abide by all the rules of a good sport for two Good Sport Sessions. When this happens, congratulate yourself because your child is making good first impressions. Other children will want to get to know your child. Chapter 8 helps you guide your child to look for closer friends.

✔	Good Sport Sessions Checklist

Step 1:	Bring an icebreaker toy and something for you to pretend to read.
	    Good toys are a ball, jump rope, or chalk (for hopscotch).
	    Don't bring one at a time toys, violent activities, water pistols, or toys that shoot projectiles.

Step 2:	Teach your child the rules for a good sport.
	Teach these rules first:
	    1. Take the game seriously—no clowning around.
	    2. No refereeing.
	    3. Let others have fun too.
	    4. Praise other children.
	Teach these rules as they come up in play:
	    5. If bored, suggest a change in activity or having a turn.
	    6. Suggest a new rule instead of arguing.
	    7. If you win, pretend winning was not important to you.
	    8. Do not walk away from a game when you are losing or tired of playing.

Step 3:	Encourage your child to attempt to join.
	    Your child should wait for a break in the activity before attempting to join.
	    If the above doesn't work, have your child start playing by himself with the icebreaker toy. He asks any children watching to play.

Step 4:	See that your child follows the rules of a good sport.
	    Plan A: If your child occasionally breaks a Good Sport Rule you have taught him:
	    Just before the game, remind him of the four rules.
	    Immediately after he breaks a rule, pull him aside and remind him.
	    Plan B: If your child breaks a rule you haven't told him about yet:
	    Immediately take your child aside. In a neutral tone, whisper the appropriate rule.

Step 5:	Have your child ask his playmates if it's okay to stop. He doesn't leave the game without asking permission of his other playmates.

Step 6:	Praise your child.
	    Do this in private, on the way home.
	    Give your child a reward if you promised one and he's earned it.

Step 7:	If your child has trouble following the rules, make a pact with your child before the next Good Sport Session.
	    Agree with your child on a small reward after the Good Sport Session. Stick to your agreement.
	    Tell your child the maximum number of times you will remind him in order for him to still get the reward. Don't count the first time for Rules 5-8.

8
LOOKING FOR CLOSER FRIENDS & JOINING A FRIENDSHIP CIRCLE

THE PROBLEM:

My son has no close friends. What can I do about this?

My daughter feels left out of a friendship circle of four girls at her school. How can I help?

BACKGROUND: How children pick close friends

As elementary school children grow, they relate to their close friends more deeply.

To a first grader, a close friend is anyone they play with, especially, anyone they have play dates with. Children begin to have special interests by fourth grade. Fifth and sixth grade children are most intimate with their same-sex friends before their interest in the opposite sex begins to distract them. You can see this in the following table.

Development of close friendships

Grade	What they do with close friends	How they view close friends
Kinder-garten & 1st	They will play with anyone. Closer friends determined by how often they get together after school.	Close friends share activities and toys.
2nd & 3rd	Boys and girls publicly avoid each other. BOYS: Start to organize into small group games with rules. They form temporary clubs with a leader. GIRLS: Closer 4 or 5 friends sometimes become a friendship circle.	Close friends begin to cooperate and adjust to each others' actions and thoughts. BOYS: sometimes exclude others from their clubs but it's only temporary. GIRLS: sometimes threaten each other with "not being friends" but they don't mean it.
4th	Best friends begin to emerge. BOYS: Small groups begin to hang around with each other. GIRLS: Friendship circles are more constant, and begin to center on interests—bike riding, ballet, theater group, etc.	Close friends have common interests, likes and dislikes, similar abilities, compatible personalities.
5th	BOYS: Hang around exclusively with a group of other boys with similar interests. GIRLS: Longer telephone calls and sharing secrets make their debut.	Close friends are intimate and support each other.
6th	BOYS: Conversation begins to play a larger part in their get- togethers. GIRLS: Have telephone calls for conversation rather than information.	Close friends really understand each other.

The value of friendship circles

Seven times as many boys as girls enroll in my Making and Keeping Friends classes. It seems that far fewer girls than boys have friendship problems. Part of the reason for this may be that many more girls than boys belong to friendship circles. Girls' friendship circles are closer and larger than boys' friendship circles. Boys have one or two close friends, which changes from time to time, but usually stays within four or five constant closer friends. Here's an example of an ideal friendship circle of boys:

> *Jeremy, Greg and Steven have known each other since kindergarten. They live within two blocks of each other and have had many individual play dates with each other, as well as with other boys they don't all like.*
>
> *In fourth grade, their parents feel confident that they can safely cross small streets. They get together as a group after the parents confer with each other on the phone. Jeremy and Steven bike ride to Greg's house and play there for a while. They tell Greg's mom they are going to ride their bikes for 45 minutes, and she makes sure they return. After they return, they head over to Steven's house, where his mom has planned to give them lunch.*

A friendship circle this large is rare among boys until middle school. Here is an account of an ideal girls' friendship circle:

> *Four mothers make frequent play dates with each other for their second grade girls. The mothers also find that they like each other. When the girls are in third grade, the mothers go out for coffee after they drop their girls off for the horse-back riding lessons that all their girls want to take together.*

Many girls fantasize having friendship circles like these four girls had because it formed quickly, lasted a long time and involved the parents. Many girls want special friends, or "sisters." The following is the more typical account I hear:

> *For the past three years, six -year old Julie has attended a ballet class. She has met several girls there, but only Ginger remains her long-time friend. Julie meets Tabitha in third grade, when they both began to ride the same bus to school. She met Emily at Girl Scout camp and also in the city orchestra.*

In 6th grade, Julie, Ginger, Tabitha and Emily attend the same middle school. They eat lunch together every day at school and have slumber parties once every couple of months. Their common interests are intellectual (they are all in honors classes), and watching movies at their slumber parties.

Notice that girls' friendship circles form slowly by adding individual girls and then suddenly may coalesce when circumstances change. Children pick each other to be friends on an individual basis through common interests. The parents know each other but are not necessarily friends.

There is another pattern that is common among girls—they don't belong to a circle of girls who are mutual friends. Instead, they have best friends in many of the activities they join—a best friend in their dance class, a best friend in the neighborhood and a best friend in school. I feel that either of these patterns are good for girls' long-term adjustment. The trouble is that some girls are unhappy unless they belong to a friendship circle.

SOLVING THE PROBLEM:
Help your child have a few close friends.

While it is not necessary for boys or girls to belong to a friendship circle, it is desirable to have two to four close friends of the same sex. Girls and boys can make good playmates for each other and nothing I am about to say should discourage you from maintaining these opposite sex friendships. However, I feel it is important for your child to have same-sex closer friends for the following reasons:

1. They will have playmates to play with in public (starting in second grade they will be teased for hanging around with the opposite sex).

2. Same-sex friendships are more enduring and dependable.

3. They will be more comfortable with their sex roles. Girls give each other more support than boys for having feminine

interests. The same can be said for boys and masculine interests.

Step 1: Ask your child about favored playmates.

Find out from your child who she is spending time with at school. Example:

Mom: What did you do today at recess?
Danielle: I played hopscotch.
Mom: With whom?
Danielle: Trisha and Joy.
Mom: Do you usually play with them?
Danielle: Yes.
Mom: Do you want to have either of them over to the house?
Danielle: Yes.

If your child does not have favored playmates at school, ask about after-school or neighborhood activities. If there are no playmates in any of these activities, follow the steps in Chapters 4 and 5 to help your child meet new friends.

Some children complain that they are being excluded from a particular friendship circle they want to join. I feel it is a mistake for a parent to encourage a child to try to join a friendship circle. Children who are not being included in a specific friendship circle are:

♦ trying for a friendship circle for the wrong reasons—popularity or status—rather than looking for children with common interests who would make the best playmates.

♦ trying to be accepted too quickly into a friendship circle—trying to get all the children in the friendship circle to include them at once—rather than trying to establish separate friendships with each child.

Mom finds out her daughter Kate is being left out of a friendship circle at school:

Kate: I don't have anyone at school to hang out with.
Mom: What about Evelyn? You play with her after church.

Kate: Evelyn is too busy with Abby and Sharon to talk to me at school.

If Mom decides with Kate that common interests are not strong enough with Abby or Sharon, Kate needs to look elsewhere for friends she can hang out with at school. Mom should help her do this:

Mom: Is there anyone else you like at school?

Kate: I like Monica, but she's not friends with Evelyn, Abby or Sharon.

Mom: It's up to Evelyn, Abby and Sharon if they want to hang out with you. Meanwhile, don't depend on them. Do you like Monica enough to ask her over?

If the answer is yes then it's time for a play date. If something didn't gel with Evelyn, Abby or Sharon, then maybe something better will happen with Monica. Otherwise Kate should keep looking for additional friends. Remember, it is not essential that your child belong to *any* friendship circle, but it is important for her to have close friends.

Step 2: Linger for a few minutes before or after school and activities.

Come in a few minutes before the activity is over and watch from the sidelines to see who your child is hanging around. Example:

Mom: [*After watching her son Alex talking to another boy*] Hi Alex. Who was that boy you were talking to?

Alex: That was Jeffrey.

Mom: Does Jeffrey play with you at school?

Alex: Yes, we played handball at recess today.

Mom: Would you like to invite him over to our house?

Alex: Yes.

The next day Alex's mother can strike up a conversation with Jeffrey's mom before they pick up their sons.

This approach works best in the early grades in your neighborhood school and also works for neighborhood activities, such as scouts or teams. I've noticed that most lingerers are moms. Moms of many first graders linger, but by about fourth grade only a couple of moms are lingering. If you're not a working parent, try both before and after school or neighborhood activities to see when most of the other parents are present. If you're a working mom, you might try to do it in the morning, before school starts. It requires a few minutes of your time to exchange hellos and get to know other parents who are also lingering so that they know you when you ask for play dates for your child.

Step 3: Arrange play dates with one child at a time.

You have a common interest with some parents: both your children will want to play together. You have found out who these children are in the last step, now try to meet their parents to arrange play dates. Although in-person arrangements are always better for first and second graders, telephoning can also be effective (see next chapter). Talk to whichever parent is picking up your child's desired playmate at school. Here's what a first encounter between the moms of second grade girls might sound like:

Danielle's Mom: Hello, I'm Margaret Chatsworth, Danielle's mom. Danielle's in Mrs. Henry's class with Trisha.

Trisha's Mom: Hello. Glad to meet you. I'm Tracie DeCarlo.

Danielle's Mom: Danielle is always talking about Trisha.

Trisha's Mom: I've heard about Danielle too.

Danielle's Mom: How about getting the girls together?

Trisha's Mom: Yes. I'd like that.

Danielle's Mom: What's a good time for you?

If the friendships form, then a friendship circle may follow.

Here is an example I recently heard of how making friends with one child at a time works, even if girls start out by excluding:

Margie, age twelve, is the occasional brunt of remarks made by girls in one friendship circle. They call her a nerd because Margie's interest in reading and horses differs from theirs. She gets to know individual girls in this friendship circle better through different activities: Mary and she are on the track team together. Joanne and Rika are in her drama class. In each case, meeting the girls apart from school in another activity leads to an enjoyable play date. Word gets around among the friendship circle that Margie "isn't so bad."

Margie may not become part of the friendship circle, but this will not matter since she has started to form close friendships and neutralized the girls' negative image of her.

THE NEXT STEP:

You've helped your child get to know other children better because she likes and shares common interests with them. Many children will make the mistake of wanting to be a part of a group even though they don't like it's members. If your child selects friends for the wrong reasons, read Chapters 12 and 13. If your child is a good judge of potential friends, read the next two chapters to help you plan play dates and read chapter 12 to help you encourage good friendship choices.

9
USING THE TELEPHONE TO MAKE CLOSER FRIENDS

THE PROBLEM:

How can my child find out if she has common interests with other children?

My child plans his play date activities without thinking about what his guest would want to do. How can I prevent this?

BACKGROUND: Developing best friends

As I've mentioned in the introduction, your child needs a best friends outside the family. The best way to make best friends is to have play dates with one other child at a time. Good play dates start with good planning. As your child gets older, she can take a more active role in planning her play dates. The next table shows how much you can expect your child to do.

Children's roles in planning play dates

Age	Ways Children Decide to Get Together
Before 5 years old	Parents arrange on their own.
5-7 years old	Parent arranges after consulting with child.
8-10 years old	Child makes call and plans one or two activities with parent help.
10-12 years old	Child plans activities, parents finalize date and time.

I have found the telephone to be a useful tool to help children plan their own play dates. When children do this before they get together, they have more fun and fewer arguments.

Conflict between children is the major cause for a play date to go sour. Much of what children argue about is what activities to do together. This can be avoided by teaching your child to Play Detective. Playing Detective is when the children work out in advance (not in the heat of the moment) activities they will play.

The purpose of Playing Detective is to get information about common interests, to be used to organize activities for a play date. Playing Detective is done best when the two children talk to each other on the telephone or are alone together waiting at school or an activity. Children show each other that they are interested in a play date by being interested in talking about common activities. If a child is rude, then this is be a hurtful, although no-nonsense way of saying that closer friendship is out. If the children can't find a common interest, they will have no idea what to do if they ever get together. In this case, they can end the conversation without an invitation to play.

SOLVING THE PROBLEM:
Teach your child to use the phone to plan a play date
Step 1: Teach your child how to leave a message on an answering machine.

Answering machines often confuse younger children, but are necessary evils for busy people. So your child needs to know how to leave a message containing:

1. His name.

2. Who he is calling.

3. His telephone number.

Skip this step if your child already knows. If your child can't leave a message, here's how to teach him:

Mom: What would you do if you called Richard, he wasn't home, and his answering machine answered?

Preston: I would hang up.

Mom: That would be okay. But it would be better if you left a message. All you have to do is say, "Hi, this is Preston." I'm calling Richard. Call me back at 555-2345. Let's try it. Pretend you're calling Richard and you get the answering machine. Ring, ring. Hello, this is the Jones' residence. We're not available to answer the phone. Please leave a message and we'll get back to you when we can.

Preston: Hi. This is Preston. Call me at 555-2345.

Mom: That was good! Do you think they'll know you want to talk to Richard?

Preston: I don't know.

Mom: Well, let's try it one more time.

Preston: Hi. This is Preston. I want to talk to Richard. Call me at 555-2345.

Mom: That was great!

Now that your child is ready to make the call, what does he say? Should he just ask Preston to come over and play? If he does, he is risking a boring and uncomfortable play date if he and Preston don't know what to play. Avoid this by teaching your child to Play Detective to find out the other child's interests. The goal is to have both children come up with ideas for what to play together. This is also good practice to build effective listening skills that will help with conversations in general.

Step 2: Practice Playing Detective with your child.

The hardest part about teaching your child to Play Detective is to get your child to begin talking. He will feel awkward. Almost any way in which he begins asking questions is good. The most honest way is to say, "I have some questions to ask you." Some children find it helpful to write down questions they will ask before they make the call. Before your child makes his first practice call, make a pact that your child needs to find out two things he and the other child would like to play together. Here's how nine-year-old Dennis and his mom practice this just prior to his first call:

Mom:	I'd like you to Play Detective with your cousin Gregory now. I want you to find out two things that you and Gregory would like to play when we get together on Thanksgiving. Let's practice first. Pretend I am Gregory and you have just called me. Hello.
Dennis:	What do I say?
Mom:	[*Whispering*] How about, "I wanted to find out what kinds of things you like to play."
Dennis:	What kind of things do you like to play?
Mom:	[*Pretending she is Gregory*] "I like to play basketball. I have a basketball hoop in my backyard." Do you know what else you would ask Gregory?
Dennis:	No.
Mom:	Think about the things you like to play that you need someone else to play with. What are they?
Dennis:	Handball, soccer, basketball. Oh, I like to play chess and I can't find anyone to play with!
Mom:	That's a good one, because maybe Gregory likes to play and you could play with him. Let's practice some more. I'm Gregory again. What would you say?
Dennis:	Do you like to play chess?
Mom:	Yes. I love it!—That was pretty good! If he doesn't like chess, your job will be to find something he does like.
Dennis:	Okay.

Step 3: Set rules of behavior on the telephone.

The two errors children most commonly make on the phone are being silly (for instance, making noises on the telephone, having the dog talk, starting the call by saying "Guess who this is?") and talking too long. If your child has had a problem staying on the phone too long in the past, agree to a maximum amount of time for the phone call. If your child does silly things on the telephone, add a rule just prior to the phone call:

Mom: I want you to make a good impression with Gregory, so I want you to be serious when you talk to him. OK?
Dennis: OK.

After practicing with you, your child will know how to Play Detective. Now it's time to make a practice call.

Step 4: Start with a practice call.

Start your child off with a practice call to someone he knows—a cousin the same age as he is will do fine. Have your child find out a few things that he likes to do. Let your relatives in on this to make it easier, or keep them in the dark, to make the experience more authentic.

Make the telephone call private. You do this to show your child how important the call is and he will be more relaxed with his friend when you protect his privacy. Make sure there are no distractions and see that he dials correctly and makes the connection. Others (brothers, sisters, adults not present to supervise the call) are not to listen in while your child is on the phone. You should hang around when he starts the call to make sure he is following the rules of behavior.

If your child does not want you to stay, leave the room slowly enough to insure that your child is taking the call seriously. If you hear silliness immediately remind your child of what he should do. If your child continues to have a problem with silliness, stay close enough to monitor the call and discourage this behavior.

After a couple of these practice calls, your child is now ready to use the telephone to plan a play date.

Step 5: Make the call for the play date.

Now it's time for the real thing—her first call to plan a play date. Help your child choose someone she would like to invite. Have your child Play Detective. Example:

Mom: So you'd like to invite Susan over to play with your American Girl dolls. What kind of toys does Susan have?

Tina: I don't know.

Mom: I would like you to call Susan and Play Detective to find out what Susan would like to play. Find out two toys or games that Susan likes to play with. If you find two, then ask her if she would like to come over and play with those toys. If they are her toys, ask her to bring them. Don't ask her over until you find two toys she wants to play. I'll listen in and help you if you need it.

Here's an example from a phone conversation between ten-year-old Tammy, an expert at Playing Detective and her new friend Linda:

Tammy: Hi, this is Tammy Gruber. May I speak to Linda?

Linda: This is Linda.

Tammy: I just got the latest issue of Teen Beat in the mail.

Linda: Yeah. Who is on the cover?

Tammy: J.T.T. Do you want to come over to my house to look at it?

Linda: Great! I'll bring my Big Bop.

Tammy: Great! I hear a dog barking in the background. Is that yours?

Linda: Yeah.

Tammy: What kind of dog is it?

Linda: She's a German Shepherd. She's very sweet and I sleep with her at night.

Tammy: I love dogs. Does she come up on your bed?

Linda: Well, my parents only allow her on the floor next to my bed, but when they're not looking, I let her sleep at my feet to keep me warm.

Notice that Tammy also Plays Detective to find out about potentially worrisome details. For instance, if Tammy were afraid of dogs, she might hesitate to accept an invitation to Linda's house.

Plan A: If your child finds two common interests:

Until your child has reached her teens, you need to get on the phone to arrange play date details with the parents of the other child. Work out all of the details other than what to play: starting and ending time, transportation, and what meals you are to provide. The more planning and concern you show the other child's parents, the more comfortable they will be with you and your child. It is tempting to let fifth and sixth graders make their own play dates. This is a mistake for three reasons:

1. One child may forget and disappoint the other child.

2. One family may have conflicting plans which they haven't told the child.

3. The guest may not tell his parent where he is and worry them.

    Ten-year-old Mark excitedly tells his mother that a boy he asked is going to come over on Sunday to play. His mother is pleased that Mark can take care of his own social calendar. The appointed time comes and the other child doesn't show up. When his mother calls the other child's parents, they are not aware of the appointment. Mark is very disappointed.

Plan B: If your child doesn't find common interests:

If the other child is not interested in talking or can't agree on what to play, have your child repeat this step with another child.

Either way, praise your child for trying.

Here's an example of how 10-year-old Ryan plans his play date with Darren and lets his mom finalize:

Ryan: What things do you like to play?

Darren: I like to roller blade, go biking and play basketball.

Ryan: Do you like to shoot hoops? I have a basketball net in my driveway.

Darren: Yeah, but I'm kind of tired of that. Do you play horse?

Ryan: Yeah. I like that. Do you want to play horse or go biking?

Darren: Let's play horse.

Ryan: Okay. My mom wants to talk to your mom.

The moms get into the act now. If Darren had chosen biking, then the parents need to make arrangements for dropping off and picking up Darren's bicycle.

Older children Play Detective in person at school instead of on the telephone. Parents still need to call each other about the final arrangements. I have summarized these steps in the checklist on the next page.

THE NEXT STEP:

Congratulations! The listening skills you have taught your child will help her throughout her life. She is now ready for the first play date with her new-found friend. Chapter 10 gives some handy tips for making play dates go well.

✔	Checklist for Playing Detective
Step 1:	Teach your child how to leave a message on an answering machine. Skip this step if your child already knows how to leave a message on someone's answering machine containing: His name. Who he is calling. His telephone number.
Step 2:	Practice Playing Detective with your child before his first call. Your child needs to find out two things he and the other child would like to play the next time they get together. Your child can write down some questions to ask to make it easier.
Step 3:	Set rules of behavior on the telephone. Take the call seriously—no silly behavior. Don't make the call too long.
Step 4:	Make a practice call. A cousin the same age as your child will do fine. Let your relatives in on this to make it easier or keep them in the dark to make it more realistic. Make sure there are no distractions. Others are not to listen in. Supervise the call until you are sure the rules of behavior are being followed. Immediately remind your child of the rules if you hear silliness.
Step 5:	Make the call for a play date. Make a pact with your child before the call: Find two activities both children want to play together. Listen in on the first call. Plan A: If your child finds two common interests: Set up the play date directly with the other child's parents. Starting and ending time, transportation, what meals you are to provide Plan B: If your child doesn't find common interests: Have your child repeat this step with another child. Either way, praise your child for trying.

10
HAVING FUN
PLAY DATES

THE PROBLEM:

How can I make sure that my child has a good time on a play date?
How can I avoid disasters on play dates?

BACKGROUND: Obstacles to good play dates

As I have said in the Introduction, I think having one-on-one play dates is the best way for close friendships to develop. Having a play date at your house is your best opportunity to monitor your child's behavior with other children. At their best, play dates provide continuous fun for both children. They allow older children to confide in each other as their friendship deepens.

The three main obstacles to a good play date are frustration, boredom, and conflict. When you and your child host a play date, you prevent these through the careful planning I describe in the following steps. I will deal with the third obstacle, conflict, in Chapter 11.

SOLVING THE PROBLEM:
Avoiding frustration and boredom on play dates

An ounce of prevention is worth a pound of cure. Good planning will help both children enjoy the play date more. I have grouped the steps by the times you need to take them:

1. Planning the play date (do this at least a couple of days before it is scheduled)

2. Immediately before a play date you are hosting

3. During the play date

4. After the play date

Planning the play date
Step 1: Decide with your child on who to invite.
Your child needs to select her own playmates with your help:

> *Seven-year-old Sarah plays with Joanie, her seven-year-old next door neighbor, two to three times a week. She frequently gets into arguments with Joanie over little things. She is irritable most of the time, especially just after the play dates. Sarah and Joanie's play sessions usually begin when Joanie's mom drops off Joanie for several hours, while she does some errands.*
>
> *Sarah's mom works out of her home, and although Joanie's mom never has offered to take Sarah, Sarah's mom allows this to continue, figuring that at least her daughter has a playmate.*

Sarah's mom breaks the cardinal rule of playmate selection. She never asked Sarah if *she* wanted to play with Joanie. To her surprise, when she asked, the answer was an emphatic "no." Sarah's mom needs to make some important changes:

> *Sarah's mom politely refuses Joanie's mom's requests for free baby- sitting. She then begins to invite the children Sarah wants. Within two months, Sarah's play becomes more mature and friendly. Her mood is more cheerful. Her mom is able to get more work done, because Sarah needs*

less supervision when Sarah has a guest over and because Sarah is frequently invited to her friends' houses.

You can also head off problems when your child is invited for a play date. Politely handle the invitation while checking with your child. Here's how Andrew's mom does this when Richard's mom calls her:

Richard's Mom: Richard would like to know if Andrew can come over to play tomorrow afternoon after school.

Andrew's Mom: Oh! Well, let me check and see if Andrew has any plans. [*Asks Andrew out of range of the telephone:*] Would you like to play with Richard tomorrow afternoon?

Plan A: If Andrew says he doesn't get along with Richard:

Andrew's Mom: It doesn't look like it's going to work tomorrow. Can I call you back when it looks like will work out?

Richard's Mom: Okay.

Andrew's Mom: Thanks for calling.

Andrew's refusal can be temporary. Andrew's mom handled this in a nice way, so that she didn't burn any bridges. It is now her turn to call and propose a play date if Andrew changes his mind about Richard.

Plan B: If Andrew accepts:

Andrew's Mom: Andrew's free and he would love to. When should I drop him by?

If your child is invited, it is customary for you to offer to drop him off and pick him up.

Step 2: Set up the play date with the other child's parents.

When you invite another child over, get on the phone or speak directly to the other child's parent. Set up play date times so that you can be there for the entire time. Only host play dates you can personally supervise. Play dates are too important to leave to baby-sitters.

Your job is to set the date and time, and to arrange transportation and snacks with the other child's parents. When calling to set up a play date, help set a reasonable length.

> *Joey, age six, is very happy to have Conrad come over to play for the first time. At the beginning of the play date, Joey's mother asks Conrad how long he would like to stay. Conrad says, "All day." Conrad's mother agrees to this, not wishing to offend his new-found friend, or Joey's mother. After two hours, the boys run out of things to play and Conrad is asking to go home. However, Conrad's mother has gone shopping and cannot be reached. Joey's mother spends the remainder of the play date suggesting activities that the boys don't want to do.*

Whether you are the parent of the host or guest, schedule a shorter time than you think the children can manage on the first play date—usually about two hours is good to start with. A short, successful play date leaves both children wanting more in the future. Ease into longer play dates after several successes. Here's how Conrad's mom does this:

Conrad's Mom: [*To Joey's mom*] When would you like me to pick up Conrad?

Conrad: I'd like to stay all day.

Conrad's Mom:[*To Conrad*] I know you have been looking forward to playing with Joey, but right now I need to know what is convenient for Joey's Mom.

Joey's Mom: You can pick him up in a few hours.

Conrad's Mom: How about if I call in an hour and a half and see how things are going?

Joey's Mom: That would be fine.

Conrad's mom calls one and a half hours later and finds out if the boys are running out of things to do. If they have, she then picks up Conrad. No one is uncomfortable about this arrangement, since the boys have had a good time and want to see each other again. The play date is not a burden on Joey's mom and she has confidence that her son would be in good hands, should Conrad invite Joey for a play date.

Step 3: Make sure siblings are busy elsewhere.
Siblings have no place in a one-on-one play date:

> *Seven-year-old Sarah is looking forward to Jane visiting with her for the first time on Saturday afternoon. They decide they will play with Sarah's large collection of toy horses. Jane brings over some accessories which Sarah does not have. No sooner has Jane arrived when Sam, Sarah's three-year-old brother becomes interested in the new toys Jane brought. Behaving as a typical three-year-old, he wants to play and won't take "no" for an answer. This upsets Sarah and annoys Jane. Instead of playing by themselves, the girls have to baby-sit for Sam. They never get the quality time each is looking for.*

> *Caroline, age nine, is not looking forward to playing at Samantha's house, because Samantha's eleven-year-old brother usually teases them both and destroys their craft projects. The live-in baby-sitter can't control the older brother.*

Parents make the mistake of expecting the older or younger sibling to be included in the play date or they leave the children to fend for themselves. I feel that developing a close friendship is important business best done one-on-one without interference. A little extra planning takes care of the sibling and avoids a frustrating experience. Here are some suggestions when you invite a child over for a play date:

1. Make your child's room off limits to siblings during the play date and strictly enforce this.

2. Schedule play dates for siblings at the same time. One at your house and one at another child's house makes it easier on you.

3. Keep siblings busy with activities that span the play date. If you can't keep little brother away for the entire time, schedule a shorter play date.

4. Have one parent take the sibling on his or her own special outing while the other parent supervises the play date.

If you have two children close in age, never accept invitations for double play dates where both of your children go to the same house to play with the same child. Each of your children needs to have his own friendships.

Immediately before a play date you are hosting
Step 4: Clean up the place where the children will play.

Children need a tidy place to place. Usually it's your child's room, the backyard, or a common play area adjacent to an apartment. Children don't like to play in a messy room, even if the mess is their own doing. A parent should pick up the dog poop in the back yard and help a child clean up her room immediately before the play date, so these places will stay clean until the play date begins. Here's how Dad gets his daughter to clean up, an hour before her play date:

Dad: What did you decide to play with Sheila?

Karin: We're going to play dress-up.

Dad: There is no clean place to play in your room right now. You need to pick your clothes off the floor and put them in the hamper.

Karin: I'm too tired. You do it.

Dad: I'll help you, but you have do to some of it too.

Karin: [*Waits for Dad to do it.*]

Dad: I want you to pick up your underwear and I will pick up your socks. Let me see you pick up your underwear first. [*Karin does this.*] I'm sure Sheila is going to have fun playing in this room! [*Dad picks up socks.*] Now pick up your magazines and I'll pick up your stickers.

Do allow plenty of time for clean-up.

Do help your child clean up if you need to get the process going.

Don't threaten to take the play date away if your child doesn't want clean her room.

Step 5: Prepare to be a good host.

Here are three tips to help you and your child prepare for the guest:

1. Have some snacks ready, especially for kindergartners and first-graders. Offer them when the children get tired of playing. This way they have down time so that games they were tired of before become interesting again. Older children also appreciate the break and the attention.

2. Make non-interactive activities off limits. Your child doesn't need a guest in your home just to watch TV or play videogames (see Chapter 2). It is your job to insure that your child does not waste a play date by watching TV or playing videogames for most of the time.

3. Have your child put away any toys he doesn't wish to share or which might be broken. He has to share what ever he leaves out.

During the play date
Step 6: Supervise but don't include yourself.

In hosting the ideal one-on-one play date, you should be in the background (except for an occasional brief chat to get know the other child, see Chapter 12). Your child and his guest need to be in or near your house so that you can hear what's going on. You stay in hearing distance. Be ready to provide a snack, to keep siblings away, or to step in to resolve disputes that the children can't resolve themselves (see Chapter 11 if this is a problem). In other words, you help your child avoid a frustrating experience.

Your child should be totally responsible for the entertainment. Avoid talking too much to the guest or going on outings:

> *Ian and Joshua, both nine years old, are just starting to have play dates together. On the third play date, Joshua's father asks them if they would like to go to a movie. They*

are both excited. The three hour play date consists of driving to and from the movie and watching the movie quietly for two hours. The boys talk to each other for a total of 20 minutes (in the car). They cannot talk about the things they want because Joshua's dad is constantly asking both of them questions. They don't get to know each other any better.

This was a wasted opportunity for Ian and Joshua, since they didn't find out how much they liked to play with each other. Joshua's well-meaning father commandeered the play date, spent a lot of money and gave a lot of his time, but didn't contribute to his son's friendship.

While your child is building a friendship, avoid movies or other outings with or without parents. I am not forbidding outings with a well-established close friend. Close friends will feel special being invited along on an occasional outing. My point is these will not build friendships. They should be done rarely and after a friendship is well-established.

Step 7: Try to get to know the other child's parents.

Getting to know each other is a good practice for both the guest's and host's parents. Exchanging pleasantries with the other child's parents at the end of each play date shows them:

1. that you care about how the play date went.

2. that you are interested in becoming more accessible to them so that setting up future play dates will be easier.

If your child is the guest, you want to be sure that your child thanks the host for having her over. A typical pick-up conversation at the end of a play date at Karin's house:

Sheila's mom: Did everything go OK?
Karin's mom: Very well. Karin had a wonderful time with Sheila. The girls play together nicely. Sheila's such a well-mannered girl.
Sheila's mom: We'll have to have Karin over the next time.

Karin's mom: I'm sure Karin would love that.

Karin's mom compliments Sheila to her mom. Both Sheila and her mom feel appreciated. This will help Sheila and her mom feel more comfortable the next time Sheila and Karin play together.

Nothing impresses me less on a play date than when the guest's parents pull up in front of our house to drop off and pick up their child—never getting out of the car. You've probably seen these hit and run tactics and wonder if the parents have any concern for their child.

After the play date
Step 8: Find out how the play date went.
Ask your child in private if he would like to play again with that playmate. This is the best way to tell that your child liked playing with the other child. Use this to guide your future planning for your child's play dates. Don't forget to praise your child for something he did well during the play date.

If your child was the host, you kept in earshot and know what the children did. If your child was the guest, find this out by talking to your child about the play date after you pick him up. Ask for details of the play date he just had, so that you can also judge for yourself. You also want to show your child you are interested in his friends and how he spends his time. Here's a sample conversation between Conrad and his mom:

Mom: Did you have a good time?
Conrad: Yes.
Mom: What did you do?
Conrad: Played with Legos.
Mom: What did you make?
Conrad: I made a fort and Joey made the cannons.
Mom: What else did you do?
Conrad: We rode our bikes up the sidewalk.

This sounds like a good play date. Both boys played Legos and rode bicycles together. They didn't just sit and watch TV.

Step 9: Exchange play dates with children your child likes.

It's considerate and polite for parents to exchange play dates. You only owe this to parents of children your child likes to play with. If your child has not had a good time, don't make or accept another invitation.

When parents exchange invitations, each family carries part of the burden for two children getting together. After all, as you can see from the above steps, it's a lot of work. Most parents value the children's friendship enough to help in some way. Here's what you should do about each of three patterns of exchanging play dates:

Plan A: If the playmate exchanges invitations:

It is the parents of the guest who should immediately offer the next play date at their house. They make a vague statement like, "We'll have to have Joey over to our house." If you are the host, make a vague reply, for instance, "That sounds good. Give us a call." Check with your child in private to confirm he would like to play together, so that you can respond appropriately to a specific invitation.

Exchanging play dates doesn't have to be exactly 50-50. Sometimes the children would rather have it differently.

Plan B: If the playmate accepts your invitations but doesn't offer his own:

You may wonder if you are being used for free baby-sitting. The worst case is when they delay getting back to you and often decline. You wonder if they only accept when they are desperate. You should not let this continue (see Chapter 16 on how to deal with this).

Rest easier if parent and child seem very happy to accept your invitation, usually accept immediately and the guest seems delighted to come. In this case, there is probably a good reason the parents can't reciprocate. Here are some common reasons:

- ◆ Mothers who have a full time out-of-home job or work a lot.

- ◆ Parents with large families, who are too busy scheduling all of the children's activities.

Seven-year-old Allen is very gregarious at school. He always has a smile on his face and is constantly visiting with one group of boys or another. The boys like to play with him. However, after school, Allen must be content to play with his 12-year-old sister or his 14-year-old brother. Allen's parents have put out great effort for the older siblings, who are quite popular. They have friends over constantly and get invited over to other's houses. Allen's parents are too busy to take an active role in arranging play dates for him.

If your child likes Allen, he's going to be available and his parents will be grateful. Make sure your child doesn't feel badly that he is not invited to Allen's house. Take the initiative. Don't expect exchange, although you will eventually get it. I find that Allen's parents will most likely begin to feel guilty about all this work you are doing and will eventually invite your child over.

Plan C: If the playmate turns you down most or all of the time:

If the family lives far from you, they may be doing this to avoid driving. In this case, you must look for children in your neighborhood (see Chapter 4). You should never invite a playmate over after he has turned you down twice without offering an invitation to your child.

If they never invite your child over but make play dates with others in your area, and if this is happening with many playmates, this can be a polite way of saying that your child doesn't behave well. It's time for a tune-up on the rules of a good host in Chapter 11.

I've given you a lot of hints in this chapter. The checklist helps you put this all together.

THE NEXT STEP:

If the play date went well and your child is developing close friendships, then relax. You child is now on the road to having best friends. If the play date was rocky, you frequently had to settle arguments, or the guest doesn't want to get together for a second play date, then Chapter 11 will show you how to teach your child the Rules of a Good Host.

✔	Basic Play Date Checklist
	Planning the Play Date:
Step 1:	Make play dates with your child's help. Your child is to Play Detective with the guest to plan his activities.

Step 2:	Set up play dates directly with the other child's parents.
	    Only host play dates you can supervise.
	    Start with a two hour play date. Ease into longer play dates after
	        several successes.
	    Set the date and time. Make sure of transportation.

Step 3:	Make sure siblings are otherwise occupied.
	    Make your child's room off limits to siblings during the play date. -or-
	    Schedule play dates for siblings at the same time. -or-
	    Keep siblings busy with activities that span the play date.

	Immediately Before Hosting a Play Date:

Step 4:	Clean up the place where children are to play.
	    Allow plenty of time to clean up.
	    Help your child do this.
	    Don't threaten to take away the play date if she doesn't clean up.

Step 5:	Prepare to be a good host.
	    Have some snacks ready.
	    Make non-interactive activities (videogames, TV) off limits.

	During the Play Date:
Step 6:	If hosting a play date, supervise but don't include yourself. Be ready to offer snacks at a good time.
Step 7:	Try to get to know the other child's parent.
	After the Play Date:

Step 8:	If your child was the guest, find out how the play date went.
	    Ask your child in private if he would like to get together with the
	        guest again.

Step 9:	Exchange play dates with children your child likes.

11
BECOMING
A BETTER HOST

THE PROBLEM:

Can I get my child to argue less and have more fun with her guest?
How can I get my child to be a better host on a play date?

BACKGROUND: The bad host

Studies show two children will become best friends if they can:

1. Quickly figure out what to play

2. Avoid or quickly resolve arguments

3. Protect each other's feelings from being hurt

The bad host finds it hard to agree on what to play, gets into arguments, and doesn't seem to care about his guest's feelings. That's why the bad host finds it hard to make best friends.

First graders Katie, the host, and Loren, the guest, are having their first play date. Katie tells Loren the rules (which she makes up) for each game for the whole play date. Loren submissively follows Katie's directions.

Although Katie is excited to have Loren come over to play, she has several major blow-ups. When Loren wins a game or doesn't follow the rules quite to her liking, Katie gets upset and yells at Loren.

At the end of the play date, Loren's mother asks her if she had a good time. Loren's answer is, "No".

Katie's view of a play date is an occasion when she plays the games *she* wants to play and is the boss. She can do this with her stuffed animals—she doesn't need Loren. Playmates don't want to come back to play with a bad host. After a while, the bad host destroys all her social contacts, leaving no one to invite. Katie needs to learn how to be a good *host* rather than a *boss*.

I will take you step-by-step through supervising a play date for a child who gets into arguments or is bossy. Through your support and planning, you show your child that her play dates are valuable. By staying in the background, but stepping in at key times and coaching, you will help your child develop effective problem-solving skills and insure that your child and her guest have a good time.

SOLVING THE PROBLEM:
Avoiding conflict on a play date

Children who get into frequent conflicts during play dates need more help. Start out by having all of your child's play dates in your home where and when you can supervise them. I will show you what to do both before and during the play date. I will tell you how to decide if your child is ready to accept invitations from others.

Immediately before the play date
Step 1: Put away games and toys which cannot be shared.

Oddly enough, putting away games and toys which your child doesn't want to share promotes sharing, especially in five to nine-year-olds.

James, age six, is very proud of the model ship he put together with this father earlier in the day. When his friend

Jeffrey comes over that afternoon, he is eager to show Jeffrey the model. When Jeffrey wants to look at the model more closely, James yells, "Don't touch!" and gets very angry at Jeffrey for persisting. This is a constant source of friction between James and Jeffrey until Jeffrey loses interest.

Imagine that another family invites you to their house at dinner time. They have delicious looking appetizers on very attractive platters set out all over the house and they don't offer you any (or worse, they forbid you to touch them). It's the same way with a child guest who is shown an enticing toy and is told by the host child that he can't touch.

On the other hand, there are certain things that your child holds dear. Immediately before the play date, put away the items that your child would not like to share with the guest. Anything your child leaves out for play he has to share. You do this together with your child. Example:

Mom:	James, Jeffrey is about to come over in 15 minutes. Are there any toys that you do not want Jeffrey to touch?
James:	Can I show Jeffrey the model ship I built this morning?
Mom:	If you show him the ship, then you have to let him play with it. Is that all right?
James:	No, he'll mess it up!
Mom:	Then put it away now. [*Mom helps James put it in the closet in her bedroom, along with three other toys which James did not want to share. She looks at the toys James leaves out for both boys to play*] Gee, you have some good games here that I know Jeffrey will like to play.

Always prohibit TV, videogames and other non-interactive toys during the play date. If the guest asks for one of these, have your child tell the guest, "My mom doesn't allow me to watch TV or play videogames when I have someone over."

Step 2: Review the Rules of a Good Host with your child.

The four Rules of a Good Host help children improve their ability to become close friends with others. I will explain each to you first, then show you how to teach them to your child.

1. The guest is always right.

This rule neutralizes bossiness and is easy to enforce. If there is an argument, for instance in the rules of a game or which game to play, the guest is right. You never have to get to the bottom of any argument. Your child needs to learn that a gracious host bends over backwards to make a guest feel welcome. A good host puts his guest's wishes before his own.

Sometimes the guest is bossy, too pushy, or needs much help. Your child is free not to invite him over again, just like the other child is free not to want to come over again if your child is bossy.

Exception: If the guest has physically hurt your child or the guest does not obey you. If the injury isn't accidental, or the guest is rowdy and won't obey you, then it's time to call the guest's parents for help. If they don't offer any help, then consider ending the play date and not inviting the guest over again.

2. If your child is bored, he suggests a change in activity.

Common interests keep a play date going well. Your child has learned how to Play Detective to find these out before the play date (Chapter 9). As the children grow to know each other better, the games they have arranged to play will hold their interest throughout the play date. However, the host and his new guest may get tired of playing an activity at different times. The next table shows three ways that children handle changing an activity when they are bored but their guest is still interested:

What your child can say to change an activity

Impolite Way	Better Way	Best Way
This is boring.	Can we play something else?	Can we play dominoes when you get one more man out?
I'm tired of playing the mom.	Can you be the mom for a while?	Lets play this for five more minutes and then you'll be the mom. Okay?

Accept only behavior from the Better and Best columns. Younger children will find it easier to suggest an end to the activity (Better), while older children are able to make a specific suggestion that the guest will find more interesting (Best).

3. Don't criticize the guest.

Again, think of an adult counterpart to this rule. You invite another family over to your house for dinner. They arrive. After a few pleasantries, you tell them how you don't like the way they're dressed. Don't be surprised if they never call you or answer your calls. Children also hate to be criticized. Your child should never be impolite. Being polite will eventually get your child what she wants without hurting anyone's feelings. The next table lists some alternatives:

Polite ways of avoiding conflict

Impolite	Polite
That's a stupid game you picked.	How about we play (name of another game)
You're cheating.	Can we make a rule that...
You missed that shot!	Nice try!
My drawing is better than yours	(say nothing)

Enforcing this rule means that you will not tolerate jealousy and competition between children.

4. Be loyal to the guest.

Your child shows that he values the guest when:

- ◆ he never invites another child in to play while the guest is still present.

- ◆ he never leaves the guest alone for more than a few minutes.

We used to know a family that would invite us over to their house. Sometimes we would find that others (whom we did not expect or know) had also been invited. We always had an uneasy feeling about this. Children are less able to share attention than adults. If two children are playing together and a third child drops by, not only is the one-on-one play date gone, but three children trying to play together often means that one child gets left out.

Another aspect of loyalty is to stay with the guest throughout the play date. When you find the guest and your child playing in two separate locations, this is due to at least one of the following:

◆ failure of the two children to agree on what to play next.

◆ the play date being too long.

◆ the play date gone sour (they really don't get along well throughout the play date).

The best time to tell your child the Rules of a Good Host is immediately before the guest arrives. List them for your child and have her agree to follow them:

Mom: I want you to remember the rules of a good host: You can't play with the toys that we have put away or watch TV or play videogames.

Molly: Okay.

Mom: Casey gets to pick the games you play.

Molly: Okay.

Mom: If you're bored, you can suggest a new game or having a turn, but Casey gets to decide.

Molly: Okay.

Mom: Don't criticize Casey.

Molly: I never do that.

Mom: Good. I know you won't. Be loyal to your guest— don't leave her alone. Okay?

Molly: Okay.

This won't be enough to make your child a good host if she never was before, but it will be easier for you to step in, when necessary.

During the play date
Step 3: Be ready to enforce the Rules of a Good Host.

This is *your child's* play date. Don't give the impression that you are a part of it. Listen from a room close by, while doing things you can put down immediately if you have to. You must listen to insure that your child follows the good host rules.

The next table will help you determine how much you will have to step in when your child breaks a rule.

Resolving conflict

Child's Age	What to expect	How to handle arguments
5 year-olds	They are poor at sharing and keeping their temper.	You closely supervise their play. They will slowly become better at managing conflict, but don't expect immediate results. When arguments turn into screaming or get physical, immediately give a penalty (Step 4). Have them jointly apologize (Step 5) when they argue for more than a few minutes.
6-7 year-olds	Two small arguments during four hours of play is typical. Arguments are be verbal only. Children remember and begin to use the rules of a good host.	Enforce the Rules of a Good Host immediately after each argument starts. When arguments turn into screaming or get physical, immediately give a penalty (Step 4). Have them jointly apologize (Step 5) when they argue for more than a few minutes.
7-8 year-olds	Minor arguments once every 2-3 play dates.	Enforce the Rules of a Good Host immediately after each argument starts.
9-12 year-olds	Arguments are extremely rare, mild, and quickly resolved.	Enforce the Rules of a Good Host immediately after each argument starts.

You'll find that with every argument your child has violated a Rule of a Good Host. Here are common violations of each Good Host Rule:

1. You find the children arguing over what toy to play with—
   The guest is always right.

2. The children have been playing the same game for a while, Your child no longer plays in earnest and begins acting silly. The guest gets annoyed by this—
   If bored, suggest a change in activity.

3. Your child calls the guest names—
   Don't criticize the guest.

4. Your child is playing by himself or playing with a child who dropped by unexpectedly—
   Be loyal to the guest.

Step 4: Enforce rules immediately after each violation.

Show your child that you will not tolerate rule violations. Immediately after each violation, take your child into another room. State the rule clearly and briefly remind him to follow it.

Tommy: [*To guest*] That's a stupid thing to do! [*Referring to a poor move in checkers.*]

Mom: [*From the doorway to Tommy's room*] Tommy, I need to talk to you for a minute. Please come here. [*Tommy comes.*] Thank you. I need to tell you something in the next room. [*To the guest*] Tommy will be right back.

Tommy: [*In the next room.*] He doesn't know how to play checkers, Mom.

Mom: [*Quietly*] Remember the rules of a good host? [*Tommy's silent*] Don't criticize who?

Tommy: The guest.

Mom: That's right. Now what can you say to your guest instead?

Tommy: I don't know.
Mom: Say nothing when he makes a bad move.
Tommy: Say nothing?
Mom: That's right. That's the polite thing to do. Try it!

Plan A: If your child agrees to follow the rule, Praise him.

Plan B: If your child disobeys or repeats the same behavior within five minutes, warn her:
State a clear, immediate, brief penalty. Example, with Mom who has told Mara to share her dolls with her guest:

Mom: If you don't share, you'll have to take a two minute Time-Out.
Mara: [*Starts to share with her guest.*]
Mom: It's great that you are sharing.

Plan C: If your child continues to disobey after you've warned her:
Give her an immediate Time-Out. Take your child by the hand. Sit her down in a chair or stand her facing a corner away from the guest. Set a timer for two minutes. When it rings, tell your child she can continue playing.

Don't ask a question when you want your child to obey ("Don't you think it would be better to share with your guest?" The answer will be, "No!")

Don't criticize your child.
("You're not being a good host.")

Don't yell at your child.

Don't lecture your child before or after the Time-Out.

Don't send the guest away or threaten to do this—in other words, don't punish the guest!

Giving your child a Time-Out that she deserves is actually comforting for your child and the guest, since they both learn that you won't tolerate impoliteness. A Time-Out also ends the argument between host and guest.

Step 5: Insure that your child is loyal to the guest.

If another child comes by or calls, have your child tell him "I'm busy right now, but thanks. I'll call you tomorrow."

If you find your child and the guest playing in two different locations, determine the cause before taking action. Ask your child (in private) if she is having a good time with the other child.

Plan A: If the answer is yes or the play date has gone well:
Immediately tell your child to stop what she is doing and join the guest.

Plan B: If the answer is no—she isn't having a good time:
If the play date has not gone well so far, then it's time for snacks until the other child's parent comes.

Step 6: End arguments that the children can't end themselves.

Five to seven-year-olds sometimes play too wildly and wind up hurting each other's feelings. They may have trouble moving on past an argument, even when they no longer care about the issue they were arguing over. I have heard of older children who gave up on their best friend simply because they couldn't resolve one argument. Children need to learn to quickly resolve arguments and act as if the argument no longer matters to them. Parents need to help them.

Six-year-old Dominic, the guest, and Justin, the host, have played very hard during their play date. They start playing with Justin's water pistols and agree that the patio is safe (no one gets squirted). After 20 minutes of play, one boy decides not to honor this and the other boy becomes outraged. Their argument is brief, but heated. Neither boy wants to play with the other. They refuse to be in the same room and Dominic is asking to go home.

You can't use the Guest is Always Right rule if the guest has broken game rules. If the guest does this frequently, and it frustrates your child, you can keep the children apart for the remainder of the play date. Your child is free not to invite him over again.

However, Dominic and Justin have been playing well for most of the play date and are in the midst of having a major disagreement.

In cases like this, I have found it helpful for children seven years old and younger to jointly apologize to each other like this:

Dad:	It may be time for the play date to end, but I don't want you boys to leave without apologizing to each other.
Both Boys:	He's the one who did it, not me. I shouldn't have to apologize.
Dad:	I'm not concerned about whose fault it is. You both need to apologize. [*Dad looks to see if either boy is willing to start, but both are refusing to look at each other.*] Okay, I'm going to count to three. On three, I want you both to say, "I'm sorry." Ready? [*He repeats this until both boys are ready.*] One, two, three.
Both Boys:	[*Grudgingly*] I'm sorry.
Dad:	That's great! [*After a minute*] Now what do you boys want to do?
Justin:	Let's play battleship.
Dominic:	Okay.

This wouldn't have worked if the boys were still angry with each other. Instead, the children quickly changed from sulking to happily playing again. Dad should also consider giving the boys a snack after the apology, (perhaps they were getting too tired) or not allowing them to play with water pistols for the rest of this play date.

After the play date
Step 7: Don't accept invitations until your child is ready.

Good Host play dates in your home help your child develop good habits. Postpone accepting invitations from others until three or four play dates in your home are conflict-free. Here are some strategies to politely postpone accepting invitations:

♦ Try to invite several different children, rather than the same child for the Good Host play dates. Inviting the same child several times is more likely to result in invitations from the other child's parents.

◆ If you want to invite the same child over more than once, do it quickly after the play date (call within a day or two of the Good Host play date to set up another for the next weekend).

◆ If your child is invited to another child's house, delay your acceptance. Example:

Mom: Thanks for inviting Tommy. It would be much more convenient for me to have Jimmy over here again, for the time being. Would you mind if Jimmy came over again? I'd be glad to pick him up and drop him off.

After your child has had three or four successful play dates under your supervision at your home, it is time to accept invitations from others. When you pick up your child after each play date, a simple "How was he?" or, "Did he listen to you okay?" opens the door to feedback from the host's parents.

Don't say anything to suggest that your child has had a problem.

Don't depend upon other parents to give you this important information without you asking. They may not tell you if you ask, but they most certainly won't if you don't.

If you find out your child misbehaved as a guest, go back to Step 1 before accepting another invitation.

You have a lot to put together—the instructions from Chapters 9, 10, and this one. To make it easier, I have combined the information you need into a checklist on the next page, with all new instructions marked with an asterisk*.

THE NEXT STEP:

You and your child have had the experience of a well-planned and smoothly running play date. After it's over, appreciate the glow from your child. Parents tell me their children ask why other children don't also follow the Rules of a Good Host at their houses. The answer: "When they're at our house we go by our rules."

Your child will start getting closer to children she frequently sees on play date. You will also come to know these other children better. The next two chapters help you to teach your child how to make wise choices for close friends.

✔	**Complete Play Date Checklist**
	Planning the Play Date:
Step 1:	Make play dates with your child's help. Your child is to Play Detective with the guest to plan his activities.

Step 2:	Set up play dates directly with the other child's parents.
	   Only host play dates you can supervise.
	   Start with a two hour play date. Ease into longer play dates after
	      several successes.
	   Set the date and time. Make sure of transportation.

Step 3:	Make sure siblings are otherwise occupied.
	   Make your child's room off limits to siblings during the play date. -or-
	   Schedule play dates for siblings at the same time. -or-
	   Keep siblings busy with activities that span the play date.

	Immediately Before Hosting a Play Date:

Step 4:	Clean up the place where children are to play.
	   Allow plenty of time to clean up.
	   Help your child do this.
	   Don't threaten to take away the play date if she doesn't clean up.

Step 5:	Prepare to be a good host.
	   Have some snacks ready.
	   Make non-interactive activities (videogames, TV) off limits.
	   *Have your child put away toys or games that he cannot share.
	   *Briefly review the rules of a good host with your child:
	      1. The guest is always right.
	      2. Don't criticize the guest.
	      3. If bored, suggest a change in activities or *suggest* having a turn.
	      4. Be loyal to the guest.

	During the Play Date:

Step 6:	If hosting a play date, supervise but don't include yourself.
	   Be ready to offer snacks at a good time.
	   *Be ready to step in and remind your child of the Good Host rule,
	      when violated.
	   *Enforce rules immediately.
	   *Insure that your child is loyal to the guest.
	   *Be ready to lead a joint apology if an argument can't be resolved
	      (for kindergartners and first graders).

Step 7:	Try to get to know the other child's parent.
	After the Play Date:

Step 8:	If your child was the guest, find out how the play date went.
	   Ask your child in private if he would like to get together with the
	      guest again.

Step 9:	Exchange play dates with children your child likes, after three or four conflict-free play dates in your home.

PART III: KEEPING FRIENDS

If you learn how to listen to your child she will confide in you and you will be able to help her with her problems. Become a good listener and she just might listen to *you* when you guide her in her choice of friends.

12
ENCOURAGING GOOD CHOICES

THE PROBLEM:

How can I support my son's good choices for friends?
I don't know what kind of children my daughter's friends are. How do I learn more about them?

BACKGROUND:
Encouraging good friendship choices

I will never forget the first time I visited Mark Siedler's house. I was thirteen years old and Mark was to become one of my closest friends for many years. I walked in his front door with him, expecting to say a perfunctory hello to his mother and then go off to his room with him. This was standard operating procedure with every other new friend I had made. Boy, was I wrong! I found myself sitting with his mom, having an uncomfortable, but meaningful conversation.

She was giving me the third degree—putting me on the spot about my interests and aspirations. I was uncomfortable because no parent ever asked me so many personal questions. Yes, I wanted to go to college. Yes, I was looking forward to school. Yes, I was interested in girls but wasn't dating anyone. As my armpits were getting soaked from perspiration, Mark was calmly sitting next to me.

There was a short silence and Mark took me to his room. I was acceptable to his mom, and in passing this test, I felt really good about myself. Mark overheard a lot about me, and when we went to his room, we continued speaking as if we had started *our* intimate conversation. I had a lot of respect for Mark's mom after that and wished I could talk to my own parents the same way.

Like Mark's mom, you can guide your child to choose friends wisely. Start this now, rather than waiting until your child is an adolescent.

You do this in three ways:

1. Let your child know you consider her friends to be important people.

2. Encourage your child when she makes good choices.

3. Discourage her from seeing children who are bad choices as friends.

This chapter deals with the first two ways you help your child. These are ways that boost your child's self-esteem. Following the steps in this chapter will make it easier for you to follow the steps in the next chapter to discourage friendships you do not like.

SOLVE THE PROBLEM:
Support your child's good friendship choices

You influence your child's choice of friends by helping your child select who to invite for play dates.

Step 1: Talk to your child's friends, especially the first time they are over.

The third degree I got from Mark Siedler's mom was a practice Mrs. Siedler started very early in Mark's life. Now is the time for you to know your child's friends better. Prepare a snack and plan on briefly joining your child and her guest during an occasional play date. Treat the guest respectfully as a child her age. Your goal is to get the guest to talk about her interests and values.

1. Start with an interest your child has told you about.

2. Be serious, but warm.

3. Be friendly, but maintain an adult distance.

4. Keep conversations short—10 minutes is enough. Remember, it's your child's play date, not yours.

Here's a sample conversation between Kelsey's mom and Vicki, age nine, Kelsey's new friend.

Mom: Kelsey tells me that you're doing your school science project on crystals.

Vicki: Yes. I'm getting crystals to grow in a jar on my window sill.

Mom: How did you pick crystals for your project?

Vicki: I like the way they look after they're grown. They look like little jewels.

Mom: Is anyone helping you grow them?

Vicki: My Dad. He also showed me how to make a poster on our home computer, so I can display my project.

Kelsey's mom discovers a lot about Vicki—her family's attitude towards school and that her dad is involved with helping her. Vicki is not the kind of child who puts off things until the last minute. If Kelsey values school work, it is important for her to choose friends who feel the same way. This is so that they will understand Kelsey's concerns about school, will not distract her from her goals, and will give her emotional support with school issues.

Many girls' self-esteem starts to decline in junior high school. Prevent this decline by helping your daughter pick other girls who will support her and help her feel good about herself and her interests.

Step 2: Talk to your child about other children's reputations.

To make informed decisions, you must learn about the reputations of your child's acquaintances. The best source of information is your child. Learn more about the friendship circles in your child's grade. Talk to your child about who gets in trouble and who bothers other children when they are playing. Here's a conversation between a dad and his eight-year old son as they are driving to school in the morning:

Dad: What does your school monitor do when someone does something bad or breaks the rules?

Sam: They get benched (sit on a designated bench for a few minutes) or write standards (a counter-educational practice of using a boring writing assignment as punishment, confusing penmanship with punishment).

Dad: Does anybody get benched or write standards?

Sam: Danny gets benched at every recess.

Dad: What does he do to get benched?

Sam: He hits other kids.

Here's a similar conversation between a mom and her fifth grade daughter:

Mom: Who are Jeanette's friends?

Heidi: Wendy, Jessica and Vanessa.

Mom: What do they talk about?

Heidi: Boys and clothes.

Mom: Are they interested in sports?

Heidi: No. That's more Cynthia, Diane and Liz. They play soccer.

Mom: Who does Ann hang around with?

Heidi: I don't know. Most of the girls don't like her. But she has some friends.

Mom: What does she do that they don't like?

Heidi: She's kind of bossy.

You'll be surprised at how interested your child will be in this conversation. Learn the names of the other children in the class who are the same sex as your child. Keep informed every few months with short discussions like the one above. You are giving your child the message that he should avoid children with a negative reputation and that other children's interests are important to know.

Don't assume that another child's reputation is permanent. Sometimes children like Ann get their act together and become better behaved.

Don't ask about popularity, since you are calling attention to this as a factor in choosing friends (see the next chapter to find out why to disregard popularity).

Step 3: Praise your child for good friendship choices.

Praise your child by speaking warmly about her and her friend. This is best done in private, during a quiet time, as soon after the play date as convenient. Example:

Mom: [*As they watch Vicki's Mom driving away with Vicki in the car*] Vicki has a good attitude about school. Do you like her?

Kelsey: Yes.

Mom: She seems like a nice girl.

THE NEXT STEP:

You have shown your child you are interested in her friends. This is sure to bolster her self-esteem. It is sure to enhance your relationship with your child even when she is an adult. You also gain the credibility to advise her on bad choices. The next chapter shows you how to do this.

13
DISCOURAGING
BAD CHOICES

THE PROBLEM:

How do I help my child make better choices in friends?
What do I do about my child's involvement with a crowd I don't like?

BACKGROUND: Relationships to avoid

Here are four common types of relationships for your child to avoid:

1. The popular child trap

Your child should select friends because he likes them and they're available, not because they're popular.

> Allison wants to invite a boy for her ten-year-old son Steven to play with, hoping to expand Steven's friendship circle. She asks Steven who he wants to invite. Steven picks Frank, one of the most popular boys in his class. Frank is the only one he wants to invite. There is no other. Allison tries three times over the next two weeks to invite Frank.

Although Frank's mother never says no, she can't come up with a time when he is available. Finally, Allison gives up and Steven is heartbroken.

Many children looking for friends select a very popular child who is too busy with friends he already has to make new ones. Avoid setting your child up for disappointment by asking yourself these questions:

1. Is the child nice? Studies show that popularity is determined to a high degree by attractiveness, size, strength, and physical ability. The most popular children are not necessarily the nicest.

2. Will the child be able to get together with my child reliably enough for a meaningful friendship to develop? A popular child may work my child into his busy schedule once a month or less.

2. One-sided friendships

A one-sided friendship is when one child takes advantage of the other without offering anything in return. Examples of one-sided friendships that you discourage:

Twelve-year-old Susan visits Diane just to swim in her pool. When the pool is being repaired, Susan avoids Diane at school.

Eleven-year-old George is afraid to say no when Jerry wants to copy his school work for fear that Jerry will not let him hang out with him.

Eight-year-old Bradley likes to go over to Miles' house because Miles has neat toys. Bradley does not like to hang around with him at school and doesn't invite him over to his house.

One-sided friendships are not good for either child. They take away time from playmates who will really like each other.

3. Poorly behaved children

Scott, age six, asks his mother to invite Rodney over to play. The two boys know each other well from school, since they are both frequently benched together by the teacher for misbehavior.

In a regular grade school class, the chances are that about 10% of the children (three or four out of 30 students, mostly boys) will draw attention to themselves in this way. Scott selects Rodney because they both like to get into trouble. Both Scott's and Rodney's parents should discourage this friendship, until both children behave better at school. In this way, parents give the clear message, "We don't want you to hang around with kids who get into trouble."

A child looking for friends may select a child with a negative reputation out of desperation or because the other child approaches him and he is flattered by the attention. Parents of friendless children tell me they go along with this choice because "Who else is my child going to play with?" My answer: "It's better to wait for the right friends than to have your child run with the wrong crowd." A child who listens to the teacher and gets along with classmates makes a better playmate because:

- He has more to teach your child about consideration for others.

- He is unlikely to have a bad reputation, so that your child will not be guilty by association with him in school or elsewhere.

- He will be less likely to break rules in your house and make play dates easier for you to supervise. You and your child will both look forward to him coming over.

4. Children with poor values or antisocial interests

Candace is an intelligent and well-read fourth grader who is slightly overweight. She wants desperately to join a friendship circle of girls who are interested in boys, clothes and make-up, but who don't value doing well in school.

Despite play dates with two of the girls in this circle, the other girls continue to snub her. Meanwhile, she has avoided getting together with Barbara, although Barbara and she have several interests in common, like reading. Barbara is somewhat overweight.

The girls Candace is trying to befriend do not value her strengths and reject her for her looks. Candace is doing the same thing to Barbara. Barbara and Candace may not hit it off, but how is Candace to know unless she tries?

Fourth graders Jay and Julian are great friends. One of their favorite activities is picking on Fred. Whenever they meet Fred, they threaten him. One day they are riding their bicycles home from school. Jay and Julian get on both sides of Fred and box him in. They threaten to break the spokes of his bicycle.

Jay and Julian are great friends because of a mutual antisocial interest—bullying poor Fred. If their parents allow this friendship to continue, they will be headed into worse trouble as they get older.

SOLVING THE PROBLEM:
Discouraging friendships for the wrong reason

It will be difficult for you to know if some of your child's friends are bad choices unless you have gotten to know them, which you learned how to do in the last chapter. Following the steps in the last chapter will also give you more credibility with your child, so that she will be more likely to listen to you when you want her to stop playing with a bad choice.

Step 1: Start by giving your child the reason why the friendship is wrong.

Explain to your child why the friendship is wrong. Keep the explanation simple. Show that other children's feelings or how they behave are important for your child to consider. Example:

Mom: Why do you like to go to Diane's house and play?

Susan: I like to swim in her pool.

Mom: Is that the only reason?

Susan: I don't know.

Mom: Do you like Diane?

Susan: She's kind of a nerd.

Mom: It's wrong to do that to Diane, because she thinks you like her. It's not fair to her and you will probably have more fun playing with someone you really like.

Example:

Mom: I know you would like to have Sean over because he wants to play with you so much. Do you have fun playing with him?

Paul: I don't sometimes, but he likes me!

Mom: I know he does, but it's very hard for me to have him over because he isn't nice to you and he doesn't listen to me.

Step 2: Make a pact with your child about a playmate you do not like.

Make a temporarily compromise with your child—you agree to allow your child to play with the playmate you don't like if your child agrees play with others you both like first.

> *Darcy invited Cory, the most popular girl in her class to her eleven-year-old birthday party, even though they barely played together before this. She was flattered that Cory agreed to come.*
>
> *Although there were lots of activities and a delicious cake, Cory looked like she would rather be somewhere else. She opened her party favor, a paint by numbers set, and played with it by herself for the remainder of the party. The next day at school Cory told the other girls how boring Darcy's party was.*

Darcy learned her lesson a hard and painful way. This lesson would have been better learned on a play date. Her mom could have made a deal: "First we'll see how a play date with Cory goes before we invite her to your party."

Your strategy is to give the other child a chance at your house and to help your child see the difference between bad and better choices. Limit the damage if the child is hard for you to manage, or is rude or unkind to your child. One way to limit the damage is to put a price on play dates with the bad choices (see the exception below). Here's what to do:

Plan A: If your child has several acquaintances but her first choice is a bad choice:

Have your child pick her second choice (one you also like). When she has a play date with choice #2, #2 may become #1, and the other child will be forgotten. It may be necessary for you to make a pact with your child. Example:

> *Mom:* Sean gets in trouble in school a lot and I don't think he would make a good playmate. I'll make a deal with you. First you invite over two other children, then if you still want to, you can invite over Sean.

Always offer to live up to your end of this pact. Invite Sean over. The play dates don't have to be the same length. For example, the two children you like each stay for three hours but Sean stays for an hour and a half. Here's what Mom says before she lets her son invite Sean:

> *Mom:* Okay, I've agreed to let you invite Sean over. We'll invite him for an hour and a half. If he behaves himself, we can invite him over again. If not, then this will be the last time for a while.

Remember, neither you nor your child have to put up with hurtful or disrespectful behavior from the guest. If the guest does not obey you, you should call his parents and have them either come up with a way he will obey you or make arrangements to end the play date early.

Plan B: If your child has no choice in playmates but a poor one :

Make a pact. Example:

Mom: First try to meet other children in the park or at school [*see Chapter 6 before you do this with your child*], then if you still want to, you can invite over Sean.

Always offer to follow through with a play date with a child you think is a bad choice, if your child completes his part of the deal.

Exception: Cut off contact with a friend your child gets into trouble with. In this case, say to your child:

Dad: I'm sorry. I can't allow you to play with Rodney. You have both been in to serious trouble together and you have lost your freedom to get together with each other.

Step 3: Be firm about a bad choice playmate.

Even if your child still likes a bad choice you do not have to put up with a child who doesn't listen to you. Tell your child why you don't want to invite him over again. Example:

Mom: I know you like to play with Sean, but he's too hard for me to take care of. I cannot invite him over again until he's able to behave himself better.

THE NEXT STEP:

You now know when and how to discourage bad friendship choices. You need to help your child replace them with children who make better friends. Now you can start working together with your child to promote close friendships with children you both like. If your child has few children to choose from, read Chapter 6. Chapters 9 and 10 will help you and your child plan play dates. Review Chapter 12 in order to support your child's good friendship choices.

14
LISTENING TO YOUR CHILD'S WORRIES

THE PROBLEM:

I think my child is having some problems with her friends. What should I do?

My child doesn't talk to me about his social life. How can I get him to tell me more?

BACKGROUND:
Finding out about your child's social life

I feel lucky that my child wants to talk to me about things that bother him. It was hard for me to talk with my parents. I was afraid of what they might say or do and couldn't imagine that they could understand my problems. As an adult, I now realize that I would have been a lot less worried as a child if I could have spoken to them about things that bothered me.

You won't be able to help your child with her problems unless you know what they are. The next steps will help you to get your child to talk to you about problems.

SOLVING THE PROBLEM:
Listening to your child's problems

Your child will talk to you more if she feels you are a good listener. She will more naturally turn to you for help. Like other things you've learned to do effectively as a parent, your patience will be rewarded.

Step 1: Try the direct approach first.

I'm sure you've already tried the direct approach to get your child to talk to you, but here are some hints to make it work better.

1. *Good Times:* When there are no pressures and you are alone with your child and relaxed. Examples:
   ◆ When traveling together, for instance, walking or driving your child from school. Don't play the radio if you're in the car.
   ◆ When playing a simple game requiring little concentration. Be prepared for lots of breaks in the conversation.
   ◆ While eating together, when you are alone with your child.
   ◆ A few minutes prior to bedtime.

2. *Body language:* Move up close. Allow your child to move away if she doesn't want to talk, but wait a few seconds to see if she comes back.

3. *Eye contact:* Girls—Look your daughter in the eye. Boys—Walk or sit side-by-side glancing at your son's eyes once in a while.

4. *Voice tone:* Clearly audible and empathic, slightly sad in tone. Avoid humor or smiling.

5. *Opening line:* Make it short, but to the point. Examples:
   "Is something bothering you?"
   "You look like you've had a hard day at school. Want to talk about it?"

"Were you able to patch things up with Ginny?" (Dad knows that his daughter has had a falling out with Ginny.)

Plan A: If your child doesn't want to talk:

Don't keep asking questions. Instead, open the door to talking about it later. Example:

Dad: Is anything bothering you?

Ann: [*Obviously agitated*] Nothing.

Dad: Oh. It seems like something is bothering you. Maybe I'm wrong then.

Your child may not talk to you when you ask, but she may when you least expect it.

Plan B: If your child begins to talk:

Talk with your child in a matter-of-fact way. Rephrase what your child is saying, in a neutral tone of voice, or ask her what she thinks is going on, until you get the full story. Example:

Ann: The girls have been avoiding me at school.

Dad: They've been avoiding you?

Ann: Yes, when I go over to sit with them at lunch, Amy tells them to move.

Dad: What happens next?

Ann: They all move to another table and leave me sitting alone.

Dad: Oh. Why do you think they're doing that to you?

Be patient. Let your child talk about it as slowly as she wants. Avoid the following mistakes, which will stop your child from talking or make her feel brushed off:

1. Trying to solve the problem before your child is through describing it.

2. Showing your child you're upset (even if you are).

3. Criticizing your child in any way.

Step 2: Be prepared to find out later.

If your child isn't ready to talk when you want to listen, be ready to listen when he wants to talk. My child most easily talks about things that are bothering him before he goes to sleep. I'm tired and looking forward to getting things done around the house, when all of a sudden he'll want to get chatty. I know that he is less defensive at bedtime. Things he put out of his mind during the day have a nasty habit of creeping up now. So now is my chance to find out, if I'm receptive. Here's how a scenario between nine-year-old Alisa and her mother begins:

Mom:	Time to go to sleep now.
Alisa:	I'm not tired.
Mom:	Try to get to sleep.
Alisa:	[*As mom is leaving her bedroom—I usually find the conversation beginning just as I am on the way out my child's bedroom door*] Cory said that if I don't give her my lunch money she won't be my friend.
Mom:	[*Comes back and sits on her bed*] What did you do when she said that?
Alisa:	I didn't give it to her. She said she wouldn't be my friend anymore.
Mom:	What do you think about that?
Alisa:	If she won't be my friend because I didn't give her money, I don't think she's that good of a friend.
Mom:	I think you're right.

Mom asks Alisa what she thinks. This gives her a chance to think through what is going on. Then Mom can give her the credit for solving her own problem. If Alisa chose unwisely, Mom would ask a question like, "What makes you say that?" in order to help Alisa think through the problem better. She then helps her come up with a better solution.

If you can't find out from your child, and you think there is a serious problem which has been going on for more than a week, go to Step 3.

Step 3: Ask the teacher.

Elementary school teachers spend most of the day with children. They're usually good at noticing when a child needs help. Briefly and in private, describe to the teacher the changes you have noticed in your child:

Mom: Ann has been getting stomach aches on school days for the past couple of weeks and she says nothing is the matter. Do you know of anything that might be bothering her?

Teacher: This group of girls has been a tough one. They're all so sassy to each other. Like no other group I've had before. I've noticed that Ann has had a falling out with Amy.

The teacher may not notice what's going on, but may give Ann's mom important information about classmates. That night, about 20 minutes before Ann's bedtime, Mom should ask Ann:

Mom: How's Amy doing?

Ann: I don't know.

Mom: Have you talked to her lately?

Ann: No. I don't like her anymore.

Mom: How come?

Ann: She's not very nice.

Mom: What does she do that's not nice?

Ann: She is hanging around with Kim and doesn't want to sit with me at lunch any more.

Mom then proceeds to help Ann figure out why the girls are avoiding her and what to do about it.

THE NEXT STEP:

You have learned how to listen to your child so she will tell you problems. You see how your patience has made it easier for your child to talk to you. What do you do about that problem you now know about? Chapters 15-21 describe what you can do to help your child with each of the most common social problems.

15
HAVING FRIENDS STOLEN

THE PROBLEM:

My child's friend has forsaken her. What should I do?

BACKGROUND: The myth of stealing friends

Friends are not objects. You can't possess or steal them. A stolen friend is usually the result of bad judgment both by the friend and your child. I'll give you an example of this by showing how Megan's friend Libby was "stolen" by Heather and how Megan could deal with the situation.

> *Megan, Libby, and Heather, all age eight, are playing together at Libby's house. Megan and Libby are best friends with each other. Heather is a newcomer.*
>
> *Heather suggests hide and seek, with Megan being it. Heather takes Libby aside and says "Let's hide where Megan can't find us. Let's go to my house (down the street) where she really won't find us." Megan finishes counting*

and she can't find the other girls until they come back from Heather's house 10 minutes later.

This is a prime example of why a good host should be loyal to her guest (Don't have three on a play date and don't allow the guest to be left alone, see Chapter 11).

SOLVING THE PROBLEM:
Dealing with a Stolen Friend

There are three choices Megan has to handle this. Only one way can turn out well:

Choice A: If Megan overreacts:

Megan: [*To Libby's mom, crying*] Libby left and didn't come back for a long time. I want to go home. Call my mom, please.

Libby's Mom: I'm sure it was a misunderstanding.

Megan: I want to go home.

Megan's mom comes to get her while she is still crying and takes her home. Megan is miserable for the next few weeks, having given up on her best friend.

Choice B: If Megan confronts the newcomer Heather:

Megan: Where were you, I looked all over?

Heather: We went to my house because I didn't want to play stupid hide and seek.

Megan: I don't think that was nice to do.

Heather: Well I don't think you're nice. I'm never playing with you again.

There is no friendship between Megan and Heather. Heather feels she has nothing to lose by being unkind to Megan and she might get to play more with Libby alone. Meanwhile, Megan is letting Libby off the hook. The real issue is Libby's loyalty, not Heather's antics.

Choice C: If Megan confronts her best friend Libby:

Megan: Where were you, I looked all over?

Libby:	I went to Heather's house. I thought it was a joke.
Megan:	I was upset. I thought you left me alone so you could be with Heather.
Libby:	No, I didn't. I came back.
Megan:	I don't think that was nice to do.
Libby:	I'm sorry. I won't do it again. Can we be friends again?
Megan:	Yes.

Younger children (until about 10 or 11 years of age) have a lot to learn about being friends. Sometimes, they learn by talks like this last one. Good friends become stronger after they successfully settle disagreements. Good friends:

1. Quickly settle disagreements.

2. Don't leave before a disagreement is settled.

3. Once the disagreement is over, let bygones be bygones.

Megan needs to confront Libby (Choice C). Here's what Megan's mom should do when she comes to pick her up at Libby's:

Step 1: Get your child's account of what happened.
Use those listening skills (body language, eye contact, voice tone and opening line) outlined in Step 1 of the last chapter to find out what happened.

Megan's Mom:	Why are you upset?
Megan:	Libby ran off to Heather's house without telling me and left me alone.
Megan's Mom:	That wasn't a nice thing to do. What did you do about it?
Megan:	I don't want to talk to her. I just want to go home.

Step 2: Have your child confront her friend.
Megan's mom should get Megan to confront her friend before they go home, even if Megan decides she doesn't want to be friends anymore.

Megan's Mom: You need to tell Libby how you feel about what she did.

Megan: But I don't want to be her friend any more.

Megan's Mom: It doesn't matter. She did something wrong and you have to tell her. You can decide if you want to be friends after you tell her.

Megan: But I don't want to be her friend. She's mean.

Megan's Mom: It doesn't matter. You still have to tell her.

Megan's mom lets Megan and Libby have this conversation by themselves. If Libby apologizes (as will usually happen in a case like this), she goes on to Step 3. If not, Megan leaves knowing she did her best. Mom praises Megan for trying, regardless of how it turned out.

Step 3: On first offense, let bygones be bygones.
Good friends always deserve a second chance if they rarely make social mistakes with your child.

Megan's Mom: [*In private*] What happened when you told her?

Megan: She apologized and said she won't do it anymore.

Megan's Mom: What do you think about what she said?

Megan: I don't know.

Megan's Mom: Do you want to give her another chance?

Megan: Okay.

Megan's Mom: It's nice of you to do that.

Megan's mom's support for the second chance is helpful. If Megan says no, Megan's mom waits to see if Megan will change her mind. If Libby's mom calls about a play date with Megan, she asks Megan before setting it up. However, if Libby makes a habit of forsaking Megan, it's time for Megan to stop trusting Libby.

THE NEXT STEP:

You should feel good about helping your child learn to settle disputes by talking them out. This is a skill many adults need to master. On the other hand, talking things out is not always the best thing to do, as when friends drift apart. The next chapter will show you how to help your child handle this situation.

16
LOSING A CLOSE FRIEND

THE PROBLEM:

How can I help my child deal with a friendship that is cooling down?

BACKGROUND: Losing a friend

In Chapter 8, when I reviewed children's patterns for friendships, I said that boys usually have about four or five close friends and some girls form tighter friendship circles. Girls' friendships are generally more stable than boys. Once girls become close friends, they tend to stay friends for several years.

Boys' friendships are generally less intense than girls'. They choose one or two best friends from their favored four or five close friends. These best friends can change from time to time. Usually, a former best friend will stay in the favored four or five. Sometimes one of the favored four or five will drop out of favor for a short period of time. This is a normal pattern that you should accept in boys.

Sometimes, friendships cool down dramatically. There are two causes for a close friendship to cool down. The children:

1. Are no longer interested in the same things.

2. No longer like each other.

1. No longer interested in the same things

Sara and Erin have been friends since the first grade. They are always happy to see each other and have much to tell each other. In fifth grade, Sara becomes very involved in riding, competing, and training horses. This begins to take up a lot of her time and she begins to hang around other girls she meets at the stable. Sara and Erin's friendship cools off.

Even best friends can drift out of your child's life. Sara and Erin are drifting out of each other's lives right now. The loss of a best friend is a great loss at any age.

2. No longer liking each other—being dumped

Josh and George have been best friends since first grade. Their parents are also good friends with each other. In sixth grade, they both start attending a small private school. George begins hanging around with a new circle of friends at this school and decides that he no longer wants to be Josh's friend. Josh is crushed. His parents are quite concerned and encourage their son to keep trying to be friends with George. They feel it is important for Josh to be accepted at his new school, especially by George. The harder Josh tries to be George's friend, the more harshly George treats him and the more the other kids at school tease him. As Josh persists, George becomes more annoyed and Josh's feelings get hurt even more.

There are early warning signs that best friendships are cooling off. There are three stages in the cooling off of Josh's friendship with George:

Early stage:
Josh does most of the inviting for play dates.
George frequently declines Josh's invitations.
George takes a day or two to accept (only accepting if George is desperate for a play date and has no better offer).
George and his mom no longer seem as happy to accept the invitation.

Late stage:
George refuses all of Josh's invitations for play dates.
George never invites Josh for a play date.
George no longer seeks out Josh at school, but will tolerate him joining in.

Point of no return:
George tells Josh he doesn't want him to hang around.
George and others begin to tease Josh for annoying them.

Unfortunately, Josh's persistence forced things to get worse. He finally reached the point of no return and he started to look foolish to the other boys by trying to keep George as a friend.

SOLVING THE PROBLEM:
Help your child deal with being dumped

The best strategy to handle friendships that cool down is to accept the loss and move on.

Step 1: Try to catch things at the early stage.

If you find that a friend shows signs of being in the early stage of cooling off to your child, slow down the invitations to this boy. Tell your child: "It's not a good idea to do all the inviting. Let's wait for him to invite you over next. Who else would you like to invite over to play with tomorrow?"

Step 2: Schedule play dates with other children.

Focus on inviting other children. This helps turn your child's attention towards these others at school. It takes the pressure off your child so that he won't to try too hard to be friends. He will have a couple of other children to fall back on for play dates and hang around with at school, should his relationship reach the late stage of cooling down.

Hold firm to Steps 1 and 2, despite your child's desire to see the other child. If you catch this early enough, your child may not lose the friend. Josh's dad should talk to Josh about who he sees in school. If Josh's dad helps Josh take action before the point of no return, George may want to be Josh's friend again after a while. If your child's relationship enters the point of no return, then go to Step 3.

Step 3: Help your child grieve for the lost friend.

Josh's dad should give him his sympathy and let him grieve:

Josh: George told me he doesn't want to be friends any more.

Josh's Dad: I'm sorry to hear that. Why do you suppose that is?

Josh: He's hanging around with others at school I don't like.

Josh's Dad: That's too bad. I lost a best friend once and it was hard for me.

Josh: What can I do?

Josh's Dad: Nothing. You don't have to be friends with George. George found other boys to be friends with, so you will too.

The pressure is off. Josh mopes for a while and with his parents' encouragement he begins finding new friends.

THE NEXT STEP:

It's hard to lose a best friend and unfortunately it happens to all of us at one time or another. There is no easy way to get over it. You have helped your child make as good an adjustment as possible. If your child is skilled at making new friends, he will take it from there. If not, follow the steps in Chapter 6.

17
MOVING AWAY

THE PROBLEM:

How can I prepare my child for moving away from her friends?
How can I help my child adjust after moving to a new area?

BACKGROUND: Cut adrift after a move

I find that the loss of friends after a move is especially painful for girls because they make new friends more slowly than boys.

Ten-year-old Josie is a bright girl who likes to read. She is very close friends with three other girls with similar interests. Her parents are forced to move because of a job change. Josie, naturally quiet, retreats into reading more books, instead of making friends with her new classmates. Her parents worry that she is reading too much and that she doesn't have any other girls over.

The other girls in her new class are nice to her, but they are busy with their own friends. Josie does well in school. After a few months, other girls are calling her for homework assignments and she begins to make new friends.

Everyone in Josie's family feels cut adrift from their friends after the move. Josie has made friends before. She has the social skills to be accepted in her new school. She knows how to make friends and how to behave with close friends.

Twelve-year-old Nancy's family never stays in one place for more than two or three years. Since she has been in kindergarten, her family has moved three times. She is a pleasant girl, somewhat quiet. Many children in her present school have had best friends for at least a couple of years. Each time she moves, Nancy mourns the loss of good friends from the previous town and it's harder for her to get to know new girls. Eventually she meets other girls in school, but best friends are harder to make each time. On this last move, she draws closer to her mother and doesn't make any best friends with other girls.

Children in families who move repeatedly are especially vulnerable after each move. They learn that close friends are only temporary. This hurts their adjustment, especially when they finally settle down in one place.

SOLVING THE PROBLEM:
Help your child adjust to a move

When I was in my teens, I fell in with a good group of kids: Mark Siedler, who wanted to be a veterinarian; Joe Pruitt, who was a smart kid with a great sense of humor; Johnny Rodd, who was not too concerned about being cool to have heart-to-heart talks with me. I left to go to college and fell out of touch with them. I still miss them today. It's comforting to know we have friends, even if we don't see them often.

There are three stages that are normal for your family to go through with friends when you move:

1. Separation from old friends.

2. Mourning the loss of old friends.

3. Making new friends.

The following steps help you to allow enough time to leave and mourn old friends. They show you how to act quickly to get your child to make new friends.

Before the move—Separation from old friends
Step 1: Tell friends 1-2 months before you are moving.
Telling friends 1-2 months before you move gives friends enough time to adjust. Telling your child's friends too soon may start the separation process too early. Parents may put your child last to make play dates. A good way to announce you are moving:

> *Lucy's Mom:* [*At the end of a play date with Melanie, to both Melanie and her mom*] I'm sorry to tell you that we're moving at the end of the month. Melanie and Lucy have been such good friends. I'm sure they're going to miss each other.
> *Melanie's Mom:* When are you leaving?
> *Lucy's Mom:* On May 1st. Is it Okay if the girls have two more play dates before then, so that they can say good-bye?
> *Melanie's Mom:* That's fine. When can we get them together?

The moms then set up both play dates. Children who are good friends will want to keep on playing until the last day. In this way, they give each other the message that the friendship has been worthwhile.

Step 2: Say good bye on a last play date
Ceremonies—weddings, graduations, and saying good-bye before moving away—mark changes in our lives. Sharing our uncertainties as well as our joy helps comfort us. Children let go easier when they exchange mementos to remember each other. Good mementos are inexpensive but have personal meaning. For example, if girls frequently played jump rope together, then a jump

rope just like your daughter's would be ideal to give to her best friend.

Step 3: Talk to your child about the new neighborhood.

When a former Chairperson of my department stepped down, his parting words were "Change is both a time of loss and a time of opportunity." This is a good way to have your child think of the move.

Follow the steps in Chapter 14 to listen to your child's worries about moving. Common worries are:

◆ Will I meet anyone I like?

◆ Will I like my new school?

◆ Will my new room be as comfortable a place as my room is now?

Talk to your child about her new school and neighborhood. Prepare your child for the different experiences she is about to have. Help your child see the move as an opportunity to meet new friends. Example:

Mom:	You're going to have your own bedroom in the new house.
Sue:	Where's my sister going to sleep?
Mom:	She'll be in the room next to you.
Sue:	Will there be a place for all my stuffed animals?
Mom:	I'll help you make one. Where would you like them?
Sue:	How about in a hammock over my bed so they can see me sleeping?
Mom:	Okay. Also I noticed that a girl your age lives at the end of the block.
Sue:	Does she like to roller blade?
Mom:	I don't know, maybe you can ask her.

Immediately after the move—Mourning and making new friends

Step 4: Have your child continue to value old friendships.

Losing close friends is hard for a child. Many children go into a period of mourning over this loss. Help your child continue the value placed on the friendship, even when it is impossible to continue the friendship.

> *Chelsea is nine years old and has been friends with Kimberly since kindergarten. Her family moved when she was about to enter fourth grade. She frequently sobs at night, during the first three months in her new house, thinking about how much she misses Kimberly. She feels better when she writes to Kimberly, even though Kimberly never answers her letters. Two years later, although only once hearing from Kimberly, she still regards Kimberly as her best friend.*

It is important for Chelsea, as for many girls I have interviewed, to think of her treasured best friend as permanent. Kimberly is an anchor point in Chelsea's changing world. She may not see Kimberly again or hear from her, but writing makes her feel much better. Sometimes best friends who are separated keep in contact. Sometimes they never write back. Chelsea's mom should encourage writing letters, especially soon after the move. Example:

Mom: Why don't you write a letter to Kimberly and tell her how much you miss her?

Chelsea: I've written Kimberly a letter already and she hasn't answered me.

Mom: Sometimes writing helps you feel better. We can decide if you should mail the letter after you write it.

Step 5: Use vacations and community resources to meet new friends.

Although it is common for children to mourn the loss of their close friends, it is healthy for them to start to meet new friends as soon as possible. Don't wait for them to get over this loss before you try to get them to meet new friends.

> *Darla, age eight, has moved to a new neighborhood in which her school is five minutes from her home. Her mother, Rosemary, is on the lookout all summer for activities that children and parents from the new school attend. Rosemary enrolls Darla in a camp that draws children from her neighborhood. Darla discovers that Melanie, her eight-year-old playmate at camp, goes to the same school as Darla is starting. Darla likes Melanie and they soon have a play date. Both girls have a good time together and soon several good play dates follow.*
>
> *The first week of school, Darla sees Melanie on the playground during recess and immediately walks over. Darla and Melanie are thrilled to see each other.*

Starting a new class is stressful for children, especially if they don't know anyone in the new class. Summer is the best time of year for families to move. This is because children have a lot of time to play and parents are especially willing to make play dates during the week to keep them busy. Rosemary effectively uses community resources over the summer to help Darla meet others in her new school. Darla does the rest. Follow steps in Chapters 4 and 5 to find and join activities in your new neighborhood.

THE NEXT STEP:

You have helped your child start over again with friendships. Finding new friends will turn this difficult time into an opportunity for your child to master one of life's challenging situations. If your child has had trouble meeting new friends, follow the steps in Chapter 6. Start looking for children to invite over for play dates and follow the steps in Chapters 9 and 10.

PART IV: DEALING WITH TEASING, BULLYING AND MEANNESS

When your child is being teased or bullied you just want it to stop. You feel like locking up his tormentor and throwing out the key. But you can't. You can, however, teach your child how to deal with it himself—and he can learn to do it far more effectively than you could do it for him.

18

TAKING THE FUN OUT OF TEASING

THE PROBLEM:

My child is being teased. How can I get this to stop?

BACKGROUND: Being teased

First grader Laura makes her classmate Kim's life miserable. At first, Kim joins in playing tag with other children, but Laura is quick to point out that Kim is a slow poke and calls her dumb. None of the other girls want to risk being teased along with Kim, so none of them say anything. After a while, Kim asks to stay in at recess ostensibly to help the teacher, because she is afraid of being teased.

Kim's mother is upset when Kim tells her about this. She knows that if she tries to do anything about it herself, it would make Kim look worse to the other girls. It would also give Laura something more to tease Kim about, and make Kim feel more awkward.

Why do kids tease? Do they pick on the child who is different just because she is different? I don't feel this is the real reason. I'll demonstrate this by telling you about two overweight second grade boys I know:

Overweight, not teased

Donald is clumsy in sports, can't throw a ball and runs in an uncoordinated way. He is very polite, well groomed, and considerate of others. He is an average student, enjoys riding his bicycle, skating, and plays goalie on his soccer team. Several boys always want to make play dates with Donald.

Overweight, frequently teased

Timothy is a pudgy 8-year-old. Two of his classmates enjoy calling Timothy "Fatty" because when they do, he gets tearful, chases after them, tells them they are not being nice, or threatens to tell the teacher. This makes them laugh.

Sometimes he says nothing, but hits the teaser. This gets him in trouble with the teacher and yard monitor. Timothy's responses to being teased have made the teasing more fun for the other children, since now the children provoke him to hit them in order to get him into trouble.

If being overweight were a reason to be teased, then both boys would be teased. No one teases Donald. What he lacks in physical graces he makes up for in social graces, including how to handle being teased. I don't find that overweight children have fewer friends or are teased more. I also find that children who are being teased don't know how to handle it.

Ineffective responses to teasing

Children tease because it's fun for them to see someone become upset when his buttons are pushed. How children tease changes with age. Children up to second grade tease by name-calling. Older children who tease use more elaborate statements. They attack the dignity of family members (especially moms, because it hurts more). Anything that will get someone upset, or get laughs at another's expense, will do as a tease.

Timothy's two classmates get him upset by calling him "Fatty." He continues to be teased because his responses are babyish and ineffective. Although only a small minority of kids will tease Timothy, others laugh at Timothy's graceless handling of being teased. The children continue teasing Timothy because they enjoy his reaction and they like making the other children laugh at his expense.

Telling the teacher may work in first grade, but by second grade, children tell me this is babyish and teasing continues ("tattletale"). Walking away from the teaser sometimes works. But what if Timothy or Kim is playing with others? Do they stop playing when they are teased? The key for Timothy and Kim is not to cry, get angry, or shrink from playmates but to learn effective things to say back.

SOLVING THE PROBLEM:
Teach your child to Make Fun of the Teasing

My experience shows that the most effective technique you can teach your child is to Make Fun of the Teasing. Your child makes fun of the teaser's inability to tease well. This is different from teasing back: Your child does not sink to the level of the teaser, but shows through humor that the teasing does not push his buttons (even if it does). Children who learn this tell me they have success the first time they use it. They get sympathy from onlookers and take away the fun of teasing.

Mothers are better than fathers at getting their child to practice responses to teasing. If the teasing is about mom (for instance, "Your mom's fat.") and mom doesn't seem to care about the content ("So what?"), then it takes a lot of the hurt out of the teasing. Your child no longer feels he has to defend the family honor, so he has less reason to be upset when he's teased.

Step 1: Get as much information as you can about the teasing.

Use the listening skills you learned in Chapter 14 to talk about the teasing in a calm, matter-of-fact way. This will help neutralize your child's hurt feelings. Find out who is doing the teasing and as much information about what they are saying as your child will comfortably say. Don't get angry or laugh at the teasing. Don't give advice at this point. Only gather information. Making suggestions too early will end the conversation before you get what you need.

The best way to neutralize the hurt of teasing is to remain neutral yourself. Be patient and let your child tell about it as slowly as he wants. Example:

Mom: How did things go in school today?

Timothy: [*Visibly upset*] Okay.

Mom: Did something happen today that you would like to tell me about?

Timothy: No.

Mom: Okay.

Timothy: [*After 10 minutes of silence*] The other kids were teasing me again today.

Mom: [*In a serious tone*] Oh, I see. It happened today?

Timothy: Yes.

Mom: Who teased you today?

Timothy: A whole bunch of kids.

Mom: What did they say?

Timothy: Sam called our family the "fat butts," and the other kids laughed.

Mom: [*Serious, but neutral tone of voice*] Was Sam the only one calling us the fat butts, or was someone else doing it also?

Mom should watch Timothy's reaction when she says "fat butts." If Timothy doesn't react, Mom continues. If Timothy becomes upset, Mom should refer to it as "the teasing" after this point.

Timothy: Just Sam, but the rest of the kids laughed.

Mom: Does anyone else tease you, besides Sam?

Timothy: No, just Sam, and the other kids laugh.

Timothy had said all the kids tease him, but he now realizes it was only Sam.

Mom: Is this the only thing Sam says to you when he teases you?

Timothy: No. He says I come from the fat family.

Mom: You know, I don't care if Sam calls me fat, so you don't have to worry about me.

Mom makes this last statement (regardless of how accurate it is) after she gathers the facts. It helps Timothy stay calm the next time he is teased. This will not be enough to take care of teasing. Sam thinks he can push Timothy's buttons. He won't give up unless Timothy Makes Fun of the Teasing.

Step 2: Rehearse Making Fun of the Teasing with your child.

You need to teach your child what to say in these situations to take the fun out of teasing, but not tease back. Your child will answer every tease with a reply. Read aloud the following list of replies to see if your child likes any of them.

"So what?"

"What?"

"Can't you think of anything else to say?"

"I heard that one in kindergarten."

"That's so old it's got dust on it."

"That's so old it's from the stone age."

"I fell off my dinosaur when I first heard that."

"Tell me when you get to the funny part."

"And your point is..."

This is not a complete list. You and your child can probably think of more.

1. Have your child pick ways to make fun of the teasing from the list above or similar statements.

2. Practice several replies to teases several times.

3. Laugh with your child after each reply he tries.

Making Fun of the Teasing shows the teaser that your child:

◆   is not going to cry or get angry.

◆   thinks teasing back is beneath him.

◆   has an answer for any teasing.

With a younger child (below third grade), you have to tell him exactly what to say (and keep it simple). With an older child, try getting him to use replies from the list of examples or have him come up with his own. Here's how it's done:

Mom: [*Reads the above list to Timothy*] Want to try any of these? What might you say the next time Sam calls us the fat butts? Remember, don't sink to his level and tease him back. You have to show him teasing is not going to get you angry any more.

Timothy: [*Reads from list without any intonation*] I've heard that one before.

Mom: [*Laughing*] Yeah, that's a good one [*Repeats in a confident, mildly disparaging tone of voice*], I've heard that one before. So what do you say when Sam calls you fatty again?

Timothy: [*This time with a little more confidence*] I heard that one before.

Mom: [*Laughs*] Yeah, that's a good one. Let's try some more. What other one do you like?

Timothy: That's so old I fell off my dinosaur when I heard it.

Mom: [*Laughs*] That's great. So what do you say after Sam says you're one of the fat butts?...

I find that one session is all the practice most children need.

Step 3: Ask if your child used the technique and whether it worked.

I always like to find out how my advice turned out. The next day, Mom has this conversation with Timothy:

> *Mom:* Did you get a chance to try making fun of Sam's teasing?
>
> *Timothy:* Yeah, he teased me and I said "So what!" He didn't say anything. He just walked away.
>
> *Mom:* That's great!

The first time Timothy makes fun of his teasing, Sam will not know what to say next. He will either stop teasing, or when he tries again, he will stop after Timothy comes up with one or two different replies. That's why it is better to rehearse several different replies, so that your child will not run out of replies before the teaser runs out of teases.

THE NEXT STEP:

You've helped your child deal with teasing without you getting into the thick of it. I remember being teased when I was about nine years old. I remember repeating back a phrase I heard someone else use, "Sticks and stones will break my bones, but names will never hurt me." I felt awkward saying it and the boy teasing me teased me about saying it, but I said nothing. He never teased me again. I felt much better when I realized this.

The next chapter shows you how to deal with a tougher form of meanness—rumors.

19

STOPPING RUMORS

THE PROBLEM:

How can I stop a classmate from spreading rumors about my child?

BACKGROUND: How rumors get started

Jenny is a fourth grader who was Elissa's friend and classmate. After a play date at her house, Elissa notices that one of her turtles is missing. She decides that Jenny is responsible, although she left the turtles outside her house, where anyone could take them. The next day, she spreads the rumor that Jenny has stolen the turtle. Once the rumor starts, most children repeat it to others who haven't heard it. Many children believe the rumor. Some are unsure, but nevertheless tell their friends about it. Many girls avoid Jenny because of this rumor. Only two of Jenny's close friends do not believe it and stick by her. Children are talking about this for the next two weeks.

Social psychologists list three conditions which help a rumor to spread:

1. The children are uncertain about the event in question. If they know it didn't happen, they won't spread the rumor. A child with a reputation of being honest is unlikely to have a rumor spread about her stealing.

2. The children don't care about how true the rumor is. The truth of the rumor doesn't matter to children who aren't Jenny's friends.

3. The rumor is about an issue that worries the children—losing a treasured pet.

SOLVING THE PROBLEM:
How to stop a rumor that harms your child's reputation
Step 1: Try to talk to the parent of the child who started the rumor

The best way to stop a rumor is to deal with the child who started it. If Jenny's mom has spoken to the parents of Jenny's playmates before or after each play date (Chapter 10), then she will feel comfortable calling Elissa's mom:

Jenny's Mom: I hear that Elissa lost one of her turtles. Is that true?

Elissa's Mom: Yes. It happened the day Jenny was over.

Jenny's Mom: Have you found it yet?

Elissa's Mom: No. I stopped looking for it after about 20 minutes.

Jenny's Mom: How do you suppose it was lost?

Elissa's Mom: I don't know. It was outside. Maybe it got out and wandered off.

Jenny's Mom: Does Elissa think that Jenny took it?

Elissa's Mom: She mentioned that.

Jenny's Mom: We don't have any turtles here. You know me. I wouldn't tolerate her taking it.

Elissa's Mom: That's true.

Jenny's Mom: What concerns me is that a rumor has spread at school that Jenny took the turtle and they're all in a stew about it.

Elissa's Mom: I'll talk to Elissa.

Jenny's Mom: Thanks. That would be a great help.

Jenny's mom is patiently and politely gathering information. Both moms are now in agreement. Now Elissa's mom can stop Elissa from feeding the rumor. Go to Step 2 only if this doesn't work.

Step 2: Talk to the supervising adult.

It would indeed be a wonderful world if we could always talk out our problems directly with each other. Sometimes we can't, either because we don't know who started a rumor or the other parent will not listen to reason. Since this rumor is spreading in the classroom, the teacher is the ideal person to intervene. If she is unaware of what is going on, it is up to Jenny's mom to alert her. Here's how she should do this:

Mom: Jenny is upset about a rumor being spread about her. Have you heard about it?

Teacher: No, I haven't, but it wouldn't be the first time this has happened. I have trouble with this every year.

Mom: The girls are talking about Jenny stealing a turtle from her playmate. I didn't notice any turtles at our house and the turtles were left out in front of the girl's house, where they could have walked away on their own. Jenny is very upset about it. Several other girls keep talking about this. The girls are avoiding her over it. Do you have any suggestions about what should be done to help this situation?

The important things Jenny's mom does are:

♦ She avoids naming Elissa—clearly she isn't going to start a rumor about Elissa.

- ◆ She calmly explains how the rumor isn't true.

- ◆ She calmly informs the teacher of Jenny's social situation.

- ◆ She asks the teacher for help, rather than telling the teacher what to do.

Jenny's mom stands a good chance of getting the teacher to help. Here's what the teacher does:

Jenny's teacher gives the class a lecture about spreading rumors: how they hurt kids, whether or not they are true, and how false stories can be believed even when the person telling them has no first-hand knowledge of what happened. She prohibits all rumors. The rumors about Jenny stop, and Jenny's relationships with her classmates soon return to normal.

Jenny's teacher used an effective approach. If your child is facing the same problem, and your child's teacher asks you what you want done, suggest the teacher give this type of lecture to the class. If the teacher refuses to intervene, then Jenny and her mom will have to let the rumor die down of its own accord. They should say and do nothing more about it. Children forget eventually if nothing happens to remind them.

THE NEXT STEP:

You have used the most effective way to deal with rumors. Rumors like the one Elissa started can make children and parents feel helpless. Learning how to deal with the rumormonger is an important life skill. The next chapter shows you how to help your child deal with being physically hurt by other children.

20
STAYING AWAY
FROM CHILDREN
WHO FIGHT

THE PROBLEM:

How can I help my child avoid being physically hurt by another child?

BACKGROUND:
Children who fight and children who bully

First, you need to figure out if the other child is a child who fights or a child who bullies. "Aren't they the same? Even if they aren't, what difference does it make?" you might ask. Fighters and bullies are not the same and you need to know which one is picking on your child so you can take the best action.

No child deserves to picked on by a child who fights or bullies, but fighting and bullying call for different responses. Decide from the following table which one is giving your child a problem. If the child is a child who bullies, then read the next chapter. If the child is a fighter, read on.

Children who pick on others

Children who fight usually...	Children who bully usually...
are disliked by most children.	have a circle of friends who bully with them.
will fight with anyone.	pick on children who are alone, weaker than them, and who won't complain.
don't intentionally pick on any particular child.	pick on the same child over and over again.
will fight at any time.	pick on children when adults aren't watching.
physically hurt others in order to settle disputes.	are cruel to other children in order to control them.
fight because they misunderstand social cues.	pick on others because they enjoy seeing their reaction.

Ineffective responses to a child who fights

Phillip, age seven, likes to play with others at recess. John, a much taller, heavier, and stronger boy, is his harasser. John gets into frequent physical fights with others. Lately, he has been hitting Phillip a lot.

John barges into a game Phillip is playing and takes the ball. Phillip's response is to tearfully approach John and tell him to stop, while the other children say nothing. This makes John laugh and hit Phillip.

As a father, it gets my adrenaline going when I hear that someone has picked on my son. I understand how other dads could feel the same way. Even if Phillip's parents encourage Phillip to fight back or send him to karate lessons, it won't stop children like John from hurting children like Phillip. The first time Phillip tries to fight back, he will lose. Phillip will not only feel picked on by John, but will also feel inferior because he can't succeed in an area his parents feel is important.

Phillip's parents would be giving him the wrong message—that fighting is okay and what John is doing is acceptable. It's a mistake to try to teach Phillip to fight. Phillip is not a fighter. He happens to be considerate of others' feelings and doesn't settle arguments with physical force. You've brought him up that way, keep him that way—he'll go far in life (bless his heart).

SOLVING THE PROBLEM: Avoiding the fighter

Phillip's dad should teach Phillip to stop calling attention to himself by telling John to stop. He should not take John on by himself. Here's how to teach your child to avoid the fighter:

Step 1: Get all the details from your child.

Once again, the steps in Chapter 14 come in handy to get the details of the fight from your child:

Phillip: John is picking on me at recess.
Dad: What does he do?
Phillip: He takes the ball away when I'm playing with my friends and he chases me and hits me.
Dad: Does John get into fights with other kids too?
Phillip: Yes. No one likes him.

Phillip's answers establish that John is a child who fights (left column of the table), not a child who bullies. Dad should get the whole incident from Phillip:

Dad: What do you do when he takes the ball away?
Phillip: I walk over to him and tell him to give it back.
Dad: Does he give it back?
Phillip: No. He hits me instead.
Dad: You are right—he should give it back. But telling him doesn't seem to work. Do you want to try something different to see if it will help?

Dad doesn't criticize Phillip for what he did. Also, before giving a suggestion, he makes certain Phillip is ready to hear it. If Phillip says, "No!" to this question, Dad should make no suggestion. He should only say, "What John is doing is wrong. Let me know if you want me to help you figure out what to do next time."

Step 2: Teach your child how to avoid the fighter.

Four rules that will help Phillip avoid John:

1. Don't talk to John.

2. Protect yourself by staying out of John's reach.

3. Play close to the yard monitor when you can.

4. Don't tease or make faces at John.

One of my main mottoes in life: If it works, keep doing it and if it doesn't, try something else. Here's how Dad and Phillip decide what Phillip will try next time John bothers him:

Phillip: Okay, what should I do?

Dad: Next time he takes the ball away, do nothing. Don't talk to him and see if he gets tired of having the ball.

Phillip: But it's my ball!

Dad: That's right. But John really has no use for it. He's only using it to get you to fight with him.

Phillip: What if he hits me?

Dad: Well, how about trying to keep out of his reach?

Phillip: Okay.

Dad: Give it a try and see what happens. I'll ask you tomorrow if it helped.

Dad doesn't try to convince Phillip that it will work. He leaves it to Phillip to try it himself. This way, if it doesn't work Phillip can tell his dad about it the next day and get some more help (Dad has two more rules up his sleeve).

Step 3: Ask later to see if it worked.

Now it is up to Dad to ask whether Phillip tried either of these suggestions and whether they helped. He praises Phillip for trying what he suggested, even if it didn't work.

Plan A: If it worked:

Praise him. Example:

Dad: Did John bother you again today?

Phillip: He did. But I didn't get close to him and he didn't hit me.

Dad: That's great. I'm glad to see you're not getting hurt!

Phillip: But John shouldn't do stuff like that.

Dad: You're right. But you did the right thing.

Plan B: If it didn't work:

Find something to praise in what your child tried and suggest another approach from Step 2. Example:

Phillip: He bothered me. I did what you said and didn't say anything. But he chased me anyway.

Dad: Did he hit you?

Phillip: No. But I couldn't get back in the game.

Dad: I'm glad you tried not talking to him and he didn't hit you. Do you want to get your friends to play near the yard monitor next time?

Phillip: Okay. I'll tell my friends.

Keep asking about how it worked. The rules in Step 2 have been enough to keep children in my Making and Keeping Friends classes from getting hurt.

THE NEXT STEP:

You have fought your initial instincts to get directly involved when your child has been annoyed by a child who fights. You've helped your child learn to do this without violence. Nonviolent responses are the safest to use with potentially violent people.

Your child will be more protected from the fighter if he hangs out with a group of friends. If your child doesn't have friends to hang out with, help him to find new friends using the steps described in Chapters 6, 9 and 10.

21
DEALING WITH CHILDREN WHO BULLY

THE PROBLEM:

How can I help my child when she is bullied by another child?

BACKGROUND:
How to tell if your child is being bullied

There isn't a manual on bullying that all bullies read before they start. Children who bully others do so to varying degrees. In mild cases, a bully occasionally ridicules or threatens another child. In extreme cases a bully systematically and thoroughly humiliates another child. Fortunately, mild cases are more common. Your child will talk to you about being mildly bullied when you use the listening techniques in Chapter 14. If you act quickly bullying will not get to be severe.

Unfortunately, severe bullying is a different and uglier animal. The usual way bullying becomes severe is that the child who is bullied doesn't tell anyone else it's happening. The most common reasons they don't tell are:

- ◆ It's humiliating and they are too embarrassed to talk about it.

- ◆ They feel that no one else will understand or believe them.

- ◆ They feel that if anyone tried to help, it would only make it worse.

My point is, if you notice certain changes in your child's behavior you will have to do some detective work to find out about severe bullying. Here are some signs listed by Dan Olweus in his book, *Bullying at School: What we know and what we can do.* (Cambridge: Blackwell Publishers, 1993):

1. Your child's school work begins to slide—a B student gets C's.

2. Your child shows much less interest in school work than usual.

3. Your child does not want to go to school or starts having frequent stomach aches or headaches on school days.

4. If your child walks to school, she chooses an out-of-the-way route.

5. Your child's books, money or other belongings are missing without good explanation.

6. Your child begins stealing or requesting extra money.

7. Your child begins to have unexplained injuries or torn clothing.

The first three signs are general signs of distress about something at school, while the last four are specific to being bullied.

SOLVING THE PROBLEM: Neutralizing the bully
Step 1: Get as much detail as possible from your child.

Use those techniques described in Chapter 14 to get details from your child on times when she was bullied. It will be easier for your child to talk about mild bullying than if she has been more severely bullied.

Mild bullying

Seven-year-old Victoria tells her mother that she doesn't want to go to school anymore. When her mother asks why, she says, "Because I don't want to be near Martha." Upon further questioning, Victoria tells her mother that Martha demands her desserts each day. She also demands piggy-back rides and tells her what games to play.

Victoria is bullied because she is very compliant. She tells her mother what's going on.

More severe bullying

Elise is one of the smartest girls in her fifth grade class. Her friendship circle fluctuates between two and five girls. Their common interests are making fun of overweight people and children not as smart as they are. Elise picks on Rebecca constantly, teasing her about her parents, calling them "the stupid family." She also tells the other girls not to play with Rebecca. She borrows money from Rebecca, promising to be a true friend. When Rebecca gives her money, Elise never pays her back. When Rebecca refuses to give money, Elise threatens that her big sister will beat up Rebecca.

Rebecca's mother notices that she is coming home from school very hungry. She also is refusing to do her homework because she says it's too hard. Her grades have started slipping and she frequently complains of stomach aches before going to school each day. Here's how Rebecca's mom should get to the bottom of this:

Rebecca: I don't feel like going to school today. I feel sick.

Mom: I'm worried about you, Rebecca. You've been having stomach aches in the morning and you seem pretty

hungry when you come home from school. Is
something wrong with the school lunches?

Rebecca: The lunches are okay. I'm just not hungry at lunch
time.

Rebecca's mom should show concern. Mom focuses on one small
part of what she has been noticing in order not to overwhelm
Rebecca. Mom should continue:

Mom: So you aren't buying lunches?

Rebecca: No.

Mom: What do you do with the money I give you every day?

Rebecca: Elise asks me for my lunch money.

Mom: Do you give it to her?

Rebecca: Sometimes.

Mom: Why do you give it to her?

Rebecca: Because if I don't, Elise says her sister will get me.

Mom: Is she the only one?

Rebecca: No, two other girls are usually with her.

Step 2: Take charge and do the tattling.

This is one of the few times I will tell you to take charge and tattle
on the bully. Rebecca does not want to call attention to herself,
either because of what other children might think, or her fear that
Elise's older sister will hurt her. Mom tells the teacher in private
what is going on:

Mom: [*After school when teacher is alone*] Can I get your
advice on something that's been bothering Rebecca
for quite some time now?

Teacher: What is it?

Mom: Rebecca's having trouble coming to school and comes
home hungry because a couple of girls are demanding
her lunch money. She says that if she doesn't give it
to them, they threaten to hurt her.

Teacher: Who is doing this?

Mom: I have trouble believing this, but Rebecca says it's
Elise.

Teacher: I cannot believe that Elise would do such a thing.

Mom: I have trouble believing it also, but Rebecca usually doesn't lie. Could you do some checking to see if there's anything to this? Rebecca also says that Elise has been telling the other girls not to play with her.

Teacher: Certainly.

Mom: Shall I check back with you in a couple days to see what you found out?

Teacher: Okay.

Rebecca's mom:

1. Isn't telling the teacher what to do, but asking for help.

2. Doesn't say who it is at first, so the teacher can more clearly hear what's going on. Elise is one of the smartest girls in the class and the teacher may have trouble hearing negative things about her.

This is a worst case scenario where the child who is bullying is a favored student. Mom has to be patient because it's Rebecca's word against Elise's. In Victoria's case, a word to the teacher should bring immediate action, because Martha's behavior is rather obvious.

Sometimes teachers will not think it is their business to become involved in cases of bullying. This is a serious mistake, because not being involved condones bullying. If your child's teacher feels this way, meet with the school psychologist or principal. Use this meeting to discuss school policy.

Step 3: Protect the victim from the bully.

Check frequently with school officials to see how they are following up. A couple of telephone calls to them should be enough. Since your child was the victim, you should have a voice in how they will protect your child in the future. Suggest that :

1. Elise should write a letter of apology to Rebecca rather than apologize face-to-face. Elise has controlled Rebecca by terrorizing her. Elise could use intimidating glances and tone of voice even while she is apologizing to Elise.

2. Elise should be penalized if she is caught within 20 feet of Rebecca. This gives the message what Elise did to Rebecca was wrong and Rebecca was right to tell an adult. Rebecca feared that telling people will make it worse. She needs to be shown that the adults can keep Elise away from her.

Step 4: Teach your child to disobey the child who bullies.

Bullies like to target children who obey willingly. Teach your child that it is better to defy the bully.

> *David, age eight, is walking home from school by the swamp, when he encounters three boys playing. One boy demands that he walk across the swamp to the other side. Without a thought of doing anything else, he walks through the swamp. The water is up to his chest in parts. He comes home with his pants and shirt muddy.*

David makes the same mistake that Victoria does. He obeys the bullies. Disobeying does not mean fighting. It means not waiting for the three boys to act. It is important for David not to give the bully control of the situation.

David thinks that running away is more humiliating than what he did. He is wrong. He gives the three boys the notion that they can control him. Here's how David's dad helps him refuse the next time this happens:

Dad: What could you do next time someone tells you to do something like that. Suppose there are three boys and only one of you?

David: I don't know.

Dad: Well let's see. There are three of them. Can you run somewhere nearby where there's an adult?

David: But they'd call me chicken!

Dad: I think that's a smart thing to do. There are three of them and only one of you. I would think they are the cowards.

Victoria's mom can teach her a similar lesson:

Mom: Suppose another girl like Martha tells you to give her your dessert and you don't want to. Do you really have to do it?

Victoria: No.

Mom: Let's think of something you could do. Could you say no?

Victoria: Yes. But what if she tries to take it?

Mom: Just say no again and pull the dessert out of her reach. Let's try it. I'll be you and you be Martha. I want that dessert.

Victoria: No.

Mom: But I have to have that dessert!

Victoria: What do I do now?

Mom: Say no again only a little louder. Try it.

Victoria: No!

Mom: [*Whispering*] That's great. Can I please have that dessert.

Victoria: NO!

Mom: That was great!

Step 5: Have your child hang out with friends.

Hanging out with a group of friends will discourage bullies. Help your child make arrangements to do this.

THE NEXT STEP:

Acting decisively toward bullying is the best thing you can do to help your child. Being bullied by a group of children has bad long-term effects on both the bullies and the victims. Your child will be more protected from the bully if he hangs out with a group of friends. If your child doesn't have friends to hang out with, help him to find new friends using the steps described in Chapters 6, 9 and 10. In the meantime pick him up after school or make other arrangements.

PART V:
HELPING YOUR CHILD
OUT OF TROUBLE

Some children have no friends. Some bully or fight. Some constantly get into trouble with adults. If that's your child, you're probably feeling upset and helpless. It's time to take action.

22
NOT
NOTICED BY
CLASSMATES

THE PROBLEM:

My child never wants to try what other children are playing. She usually goes off and stays by herself. What can I do to help?

BACKGROUND: Children who hold back

Some children without friends have a lot to offer others but hold back and don't try to join others at play. These children have two things in common:

1. Their behavior keeps them from being noticed by their classmates.

2. They can be very frustrating for parents because they usually refuse to try new things.

There are three behavior patterns you need to look for. The next table will help you determine if one of these patterns is keeping your child from being noticed.

Behavior which keep children from being noticed

Shy behavior	Worried behavior	Sad behavior
Can't speak in public	Can't start new things	Can't get motivated
1. doesn't approach new children	1. constantly asks for reassurance	1. had close friends but lost them
2. waits for others to initiate friendship	2. has to be perfect or is reluctant to participate	2. has lost interest in most play activities
3. doesn't know how to make friends	3. is unable to relax	3. is less energetic than age mates
4. is reluctant to try new things	4. constantly struggles with you	4. rarely smiles or shows pleasure
	5. is reluctant to try new things	5. is reluctant to try new things

Notice that children who act shy, worried, or sad have many differences, but they are all reluctant to try new things.

The child who acts shy

Deborah, age eight, always hangs back around her classmates, although she is a chatterbox at home. It's the second month of school and she has not said a word in her second grade class. Initially, the other girls ask if she wants to join in. She silently shakes her head "no." She is not familiar with many of the games the girls play, although she is one of the fastest runners of all the girls. They are busy having fun, so they soon give up and stop noticing her. She seems content to play by herself.

Deborah's quiet, cautious temperament is the main reason she acts shy. She also doesn't think that others will value what she has to say. She has always been very slow to warm up to new situations although as she grows older this is much less true. Studies show that shy children know little about how to make friends or how to solve social problems.

Children who are worried

Fears and worries are a normal part of growing up for many children. The next table lists common fears and typical ages they occur.

Common fears of childhood

Common fear	Typical age range
Strangers	6-9 months old
Separation, being alone	1- 3 years old
Dark, monsters	4-8 years old
Natural disasters	8-12 years old

Studies report up to 90% of children have at least one of these fears while growing up. These fears do not usually interfere with friendships. Be concerned when your child's fears depart from this either by being unusual, especially severe, lasting past the periods indicated above, or interfering with activities which other children do at the same age. If any of these conditions applies, then your child may have anxiety problems.

Katie is nine years old and afraid to go to sleep by herself. She adamantly refuses to go to other girls' houses for sleep-overs. One time she tried to stay over at Evelyn's house for a birthday sleep-over but at 10 o'clock that night she telephoned her parents to pick her up. The other girls are getting to know each other well and forming friendship circles. Katie is missing out on this because of her fears.

Katie's parents need to judge whether Katie's fear is keeping her from being a part of a friendship circle. Sleep-overs are an important part of joining these.

Chris is 11 years old (going on 30). His parents describe him as a constant worrier. When his gym teacher begins to instruct the class on a new game, Chris becomes very agitated and fidgety. The child standing next to him hears him mutter, "I don't get it. The kids are going to make fun

*of me." Chris' worry about failure distracts him from
listening to the rules of the game. When it comes time to
start the game, Chris begins to cry and walk away.*

Chris has to do things perfectly. He lets this worry spoil a game. He is constantly complaining about stomach aches, headaches, or other worries. A common, but ineffective approach I've seen parents use is to try to convince the worried child that there is nothing to worry about. This only deepens the worry. The best approach is to get the worried child to try new things without trying to convince him first. Talking about exactly what is to happen sometimes helps. As he does more things, he will worry less about doing them.

The sad child

Many friendless children are lonely and sad because they have no one to play with. Their sadness disappears, once they are taught how to make friends. Other friendless children have had friends in the past but don't have friends now, because they are overwhelmed with other problems.

*William's fourth grade teacher describes him as
inattentive and quiet. Most of his classmates don't know
he's around. His mother sees his grades slip slowly over the
past three years from C's to D's. He has stomach aches
whenever there is a test at school. Both parents notice that
William is always tired and lacks the energy to do things,
including playing with other children.*

*His father frequently picks on him, calling him lazy.
William is his only son and is a disappointment to his
father. When William's mom brings him in for a
comprehensive evaluation at a mental health clinic, he
reports thinking about killing himself. This surprises his
mother because he never has said anything like that to her.*

Sometimes children become sad for reasons which their parents don't understand. Sadness in children is very hard for adults to notice. Parents will feel it's just part of the way they are. Teachers, who usually notice children's problems, will not notice because they blend into the woodwork and don't cause any problems to others. William's parents and teacher misinterpreted his sadness as laziness and inattentiveness. Childhood should be a basically happy time. If it's not, then something is wrong.

A child who is sad can appear lethargic, cranky, or irritable most of the day. Other symptoms are significant weight loss or gain, trouble sleeping or sleeping too much, chronic fatigue, and trouble making decisions.

The sad child may admit to thinking about suicide. Take children who talk about killing themselves seriously, if they also have some of the other symptoms I have mentioned. If your child appears sad, consult a mental health professional for an evaluation of your child's problems.

SOLVING THE PROBLEM:
Getting your child to try new activities

Shy, worried or sad children don't want to do things. They're not sure they want to play baseball or learn how to swim. Parents I know who successfully manage a child with one of these problems, don't listen to this. They teach the worried child to *worry* less and *do* more. Here's how:

Step 1: Pick an easy activity at first.

Pick something easy for your child to try first. If your child is hesitant to go to camp, try a two hour class, working up to a day camp. If your child is hesitant to spend the whole night at someone's house, try a couple of hours at first (asking the host's parents if this is okay). Example:

Katie's Mom: Thanks for inviting Katie over to Evelyn's sleep-over. I'd really like her to go, but she says she's afraid to sleep at someone else's house.

Evelyn's Mom: Oh, that's too bad.

Katie's Mom: Could she come for part of it? When she gets there, she might want to stay for the whole night, but I'd be glad to pick her up if she doesn't.

Evelyn's Mom: That would be okay.

Katie's Mom: I really appreciate this. How late can I call to see if she needs me to pick her up?

Evelyn's Mom: We go to bed at 11:00, so any time before then would be fine.

Katie's Mom: That would be great. Thanks a lot.

Step 2: Make a Pact.

Chris's mom does not allow Chris to make the decision to start a new activity, since whatever the activity, the answer will be "no" Instead she sets up a pact with Chris:

Chris: I don't want to go to sports camp.

Mom: Why not?

Chris: Because it will be boring.

Mom: I want you to try it for Monday and Tuesday. If it's boring, you can tell me at the end of each day and we'll think about doing something else after Tuesday.

Similarly, Katie's mom has her stay for part of the sleep-over:

Mom: Do you want to go to Evelyn's sleep-over?

Katie: Yes, but I'm afraid to sleep by myself.

Mom: I think you can do it. I want you to try. I've talked to Evelyn's mom and she says it's okay if I call at 10:30 and talk to you. You can tell me how things are going when I call.

Katie: Call me at 10:00.

Mom: Okay. I'll call you at 10:00.

Step 3: Evaluate the activity.

When she picks him up from sports camp on Monday, Chris's mom wants to find out if Chris enjoyed himself. But first, she waits a little while to see if Chris will say something about it. She uses the listening techniques in Chapter 14. She knows Chris is most likely to talk about camp while it is still fresh in his mind. She waits for it to happen during the car ride home. If it doesn't, then she tries a couple of leading questions:

Mom:	How was camp today—interesting or boring?
Chris:	It was interesting.
Mom:	Good. We will do it again tomorrow. That's when we will decide whether you will continue to attend.

If Chris likes sports camp, then she stops the appraisals and has Chris finish out the week. If Chris doesn't like camp, then he stops attending.

Similarly, Katie's mom calls at 10:00. She asks Katie whether she's having fun and avoids questions about her fear.

Plan A: If she says she'd like to come home:

Pick her up and bring her back home, apologizing to Evelyn's mother. Here's how she handles this:

Mom:	Are you having fun?
Katie:	Yes. But I'm still worried I might get scared later.
Mom:	Let me talk to Evelyn's mom.
Evelyn's Mom:	Hi. What's going on?
Katie's Mom:	Katie's not sure she can stay tonight. I'll pick her in about 20 minutes.
Evelyn's Mom:	That's fine.
Katie's Mom:	I'm sorry to cause you so much trouble. Thanks for being so understanding.

Katie's mom picks her up and praises her for staying as long as she did.

Plan B: If says she'd like to stay:

Praise her for staying. You will have to repeat Steps 1-3 several times before you change your child's behavior.

THE NEXT STEP:

It's hard for most parents to keep after their child to try new things, but you've done it. You have helped your child try new things. You also know the signs which indicate you should seek professional help for your child. Your child will suffer less in the long run. You are now ready to go back to Parts I and II to help your child make friends.

23
OVERCOMING HYPERACTIVE BEHAVIOR

THE PROBLEM:

My child constantly acts without thinking and quickly alienates playmates. What can I do?

My child doesn't seem to be able to stick to playing games and activities like other children his age. What can I do?

BACKGROUND:
The child with Attention-Deficit/Hyperactivity Disorder

Eleven-year-old Gus gets C's and D's in school, despite seeming quite bright. He frequently calls out in class and his messy schoolwork annoys his teacher.

He is friendly and outgoing with other boys and always has a high energy level. He talks easily with anyone. After boys know him for a while, he begins to get on their nerves. He is the first to point out when they are playing badly. He sometimes has trouble waiting his turn and he will leave in the middle of a game.

Gus has Attention-Deficit/Hyperactivity Disorder (ADHD). Its major symptoms are:

✔	Major symptoms of ADHD
	At least six of the following:
	1. often fails to give close attention to details or makes careless mistakes in schoolwork or other activities
	2. often has difficulty sustaining attention in tasks or play activities
	3. often does not seem to listen when spoken to directly
	4. often does not follow through on parent's requests
	5. often has difficulty organizing tasks or activities
	6. often avoids tasks that require sustained mental effort (such as schoolwork)
	7. often loses things necessary for tasks or activities
	8. often easily distracted
	9. often forgetful
	and/or at least six of the following:
	1. often fidgets with hands or feet or squirms in seat
	2. often leaves seat in situations where remaining seated is expected
	3. often runs about or climbs excessively in situations in which it is inappropriate
	4. often has difficulty playing quietly
	5. often on the go or often acts as if driven by a motor
	6. often talks excessively
	7. often blurts out answers before questions have been completed
	8. often has difficulty waiting turn
	9. often interrupts or intrudes on others

- based on the Diagnostic and Statistical Manual of Mental Disorders (4th edition). Washington, DC: American Psychiatric Association, 1994.

ADHD has two major effects on Gus:

1. It limits his ability to concentrate on activities, especially those that last for a long time.

2. It decreases his self-control. Gus can't take turns, barges into things without knowing what is going on, and alienates others with his impulsive behavior. He teases others without thinking and is teased in retaliation.

About 50% of children with ADHD have difficulties making and keeping friends. About 60% of them talk back to adults or fight with others (see Chapters 25 and 26 to deal with these problems). Children with ADHD find it especially hard to respect the rights of others during competitive games.

> *Gus tries to join a group of toughs playing basketball. He doesn't try to figure out what they're playing. He just barges in. He points out that one boy made a stupid move. He points out when another boy is out of bounds. The boys decide it would be more fun to pin him on the ground. Gus gets the message that he should not be in the game. When he gets home, he tells his dad what the boys did to him. His dad enrolls him in a karate class.*

Poor impulse control makes activities like karate an especially bad choice for children like Gus. He should learn how to avoid boys who fight, to stay out of fights, to choose playmates wisely, to make a good first impression and to be a good sport, instead of learning that he needs to defend himself.

SOLVING THE PROBLEM: Dealing with ADHD

Although ADHD prevented Gus from learning social graces, he can be taught these skills. Gus's parents need to take steps to deal with his ADHD and to teach him the skills he needs.

Step 1: Get a proper evaluation.

If you suspect your child has ADHD, have your child evaluated by a child psychologist or psychiatrist. Because ADHD affects a child's ability to concentrate for long periods of time, symptoms are often missed during a brief interview with the child. Currently, the best way to diagnose ADHD is with an interview with you and checklists given to both you and your child's teachers.

Step 2: Get treatment if your child needs it.

Children with ADHD are as different from one another as any other children. Some children with ADHD have difficulty listening to parents and teachers, do poorly in school and have few or no friends, while others show few of these problems. The treatments most effective in meeting these needs are, in order of importance:

1. Stimulant medication.
A Child Psychiatrist or Pediatrician determines if medication will help your child. Stimulants, such as Ritalin, help school performance for about 70% of children with ADHD. Stimulants help the friendships of most children with ADHD by strengthening their ability to attend to what other children are saying, sustain their interest in playing games and control their impulses.

2. Parent training.
A professional helps teach you skills that will help your child obey you and his teachers better, if these are problems.

3. Social skills training.
Your child is helped in a group of at least four other children to learn the social graces taught in this book. I have found that the approaches in this book work well for the child with ADHD.

Step 3: Chose play activities that match your child's attention span.

Some children with ADHD can't pay attention to more complicated games or sports in which there is a lot of waiting, such as baseball.

- ◆ Stick to simple games.

- ◆ Plan play experiences shorter than your child's attention span.

For example, if your child cannot attend to activities longer than one hour, arrange for activities and play dates that last about 45 minutes. If medication helps your child attend longer, talk to your prescribing physician about giving your child his medication before playing.

Step 4: Help your child choose playmates wisely.

Children with ADHD are usually one to two years behind other children their age in their understanding of social graces, even when they are intellectually bright. For this reason, it is okay to let them play with peers who are a year or so younger.

Children with ADHD are high energy and naturally gravitate together. This happens either by choice or out of desperation, after they find that no one else will play with them. Discourage friendships with other children with ADHD, because two children with ADHD:

- ◆ Are more difficult for parents to manage on play dates.

- ◆ Sometimes lack the voice of reason and impulsively try dangerous and inappropriate activities. Follow the steps of Chapters 12 and 13 if you need to discourage this friendship.

THE NEXT STEP:

If you have sought professional help for your child, you have taken the first step in helping your child overcome problems caused by ADHD. The next chapter will help you to repair your child's reputation among classmates before you go on to teaching your child new skills to make and keep friends in Parts I and II.

24
IMPROVING YOUR CHILD'S BAD REPUTATION

THE PROBLEM:

Why are other children so mean to my child?
Why doesn't my child realize that he drives others away?
How can I help my child avoid more social disasters?
How can I keep my child from alienating teachers and other adults?

BACKGROUND: The child who is avoided

Three girls are playing Chinese jump rope and don't want seven-year-old Wendy in their game. Wendy tells the teacher. Reluctantly, they let her play. She cheats and won't give up her turn. When they insist that someone else go next, Wendy pouts and says, "I won't be your friend."

Wendy's way of making the other girls play with her has the girls talking when she's not around. They tell each other how bossy she is and how she cheats. The girls do not want to play with her.

Starting in second grade, your child has a public image among her classmates. Part of her public image depends on how she treats her classmates. Children who are liked and accepted by others know to follow the rules of a game, how to try to join a game politely (Chapter 6), how to be a good sport (Chapter 7) and how to be a good host on a play date (Chapter 11). Children who break these social rules have few or no friends and develop a negative reputation.

How children get a negative reputation

Wendy hasn't learned skills that make her fun to play with. Instead, she spoils the fun for others. Here's how her reputation spreads:

1. She upsets her classmates. They console each other by talking about how she upsets them. They try to avoid her.

2. She has been justly accused enough times that others jump to conclusions and she is sometimes unjustly accused of cheating.

3. Her classmates remember the times she spoiled their play but are slow to notice any improvements. Her negative reputation is hard to change.

Sometimes parents tell me that their child is avoided at school as Wendy is, but has satisfactory play dates. When we talk more about the details of these play dates, I find:

1. Their child has a playmate who lets her be the boss, or

2. Their child spends most of the play date in activities such as videogames and watching TV (barely talking to her guest).

Eight-year-old Georgia is avoided by her classmates at school, which is outside her neighborhood. She joins a Girl Scout troop in her neighborhood. At scout meetings, she does the same things that make children avoid her at school. The troop only meets twice a month. The other children put up with her.

Thinking Georgia's school is to blame for her lack of friends, Georgia's mom, Delia transfers her to the neighborhood school, attended by most of the Girl Scouts. Georgia begins to earn a negative reputation at her new school. The children in her troop see her every school day. Now the girls in the scout troop no longer tolerate her—no one wants to be in an activity with her. Georgia no longer wants to attend troop meetings, because she feels that no one likes her.

Increased contact with the girls and her poor social skills worsen Georgia's social life. Georgia's negative reputation has an impact on Delia's relationship with the other parents:

> *Delia makes one play date after another for Georgia, but Georgia is no fun to play with. She has to have things her own way, argues with other children constantly and insults them. She alienates one child after another, until Delia has no more children to invite to play with her. The other parents avoid Delia fearing she will ask for play dates with their children, which they will have to decline.*

Delia's efforts to find play dates would have been effective if Georgia was a good playmate. Instead, Georgia's behavior isolates Delia's from the other parents.

The best way to help the child with a negative reputation is to teach skills that will make her a better playmate. Georgia cannot change her reputation by herself. Delia needs to be patient and do some temporary damage control.

SOLVING THE PROBLEM:
Temporary damage control

It takes a while to teach the new skills described in the earlier chapters of this book to your child. While you are doing this, minimize further damage to your child's reputation. Here are three steps to take right away.

Step 1: Encourage your child to lay low.

Your child is unaware of appropriate ways of making and keeping friends and playing with others. Take any pressure off your child to be accepted by the children that are avoiding her, until you teach her the skills she needs to have. If your child stops making social errors, eventually the other children will forget, and her negative reputation will die down. During this time:

Don't expose your child to playgrounds or unsupervised group activities.

Don't encourage your child to make new friends.

Don't make first play dates with new children.

Don't continue having play dates with children who get into arguments with your child.

—until after you have followed the steps in Chapters 6 through 11.

If your child already has a negative reputation with the children she knows, try the steps in these chapters with children who don't know her. While your child is learning how to make friends with children who don't know about her reputation, she is letting her reputation die down among those who do.

Step 2: Decline invitations for activities which you know will be disasters.

Declining an invitation won't damage your child's reputation as much as letting her join an activity in which she alienates others.

> *Candy, a second grader, accepts an invitation to a classmate's house for a sleep-over. She irritates the other girls by constantly talking and not letting others speak. She keeps the other girls awake until the wee hours of the morning, despite their repeated requests to go to sleep.*

Don't tell those who invite your child why she can't go. "Thanks for inviting Candy, but we're on a tight schedule right now," will do. Don't burn any bridges, so that when your child is ready to handle these situations, these potential friends will be available.

Step 3: Offer to help supervise your child.

An alternative strategy to having your child lay low is to help supervise your child.

> *Eight-year-old Benjamin spends a scout overnight camp-out with a group of four other boys. The other boys are delighted to be with each other. As the evening wears on, the boys begin telling ghost stories. Benjamin interrupts them constantly with silly statements and irrelevant remarks. The other boys become annoyed, but remain polite as long as they can.*

*Eventually, Benjamin becomes bored and jumps onto
another unsuspecting boy and hurts him. The boys are so
outraged at this, they begin teasing Benjamin, and tell him
they wish he would go home. As Benjamin continues his
rowdy behavior, the other boys become more nasty.
Eventually, Benjamin can't take the other boys' uniting
against him and asks to leave.*

Benjamin's mother can't reasonably ask the scout leader to
supervise him. She has two choices for scout events: either decline
the invitation or help supervise (acting as a parent-helper). If she
chooses to supervise, she should make sure that Benjamin follows
the instructions of adults and respects the other children.

Scout leaders and team coaches are usually glad for extra help.
However, you need to request to supervise your own child, so they
will put you nearby. Some scout leaders need to be told a little more
about your child's problem for them to allow you to sit in, because
they are used to running meetings without other parents around.
Here's how you approach this:

Mom: My daughter is going through a phase now when
she is having difficulty listening. Is it okay if I sit
in and make sure that she listens to you?

Scout Leader: Okay, but I'd like you to sit behind the girls so
they can concentrate on what they're doing.

Mom: Thanks a lot. I like your program, and I just want
to make sure my daughter gets the most out of it.

THE NEXT STEP:

You have helped your child control the damage to his reputation.
Take heart. Your child's reputation will eventually improve. His
social life will also improve if you teach him needed skills described
in Part II. However, this will take time and you have just begun to
pave the way for friendships.

If your child is being teased, immediately follow the steps in
Chapter 18. If your child has difficulty listening to teachers and
coaches, read the next chapter. If he hurts or is cruel to others, then
you need the help in Chapter 26 or 27.

25
WORKING WITH ADULTS WHO HAVE TROUBLE WITH YOUR CHILD

THE PROBLEM:

How can I stop my child from talking back to adults?
How can I get my child to obey her teacher?
How can I stop an adult supervisor from picking on my child?

BACKGROUND:
Working with adults who have trouble with your child

If a teacher is interesting and the material pitched to their level of understanding, most children sit quietly and listen. A few children don't and challenge the supervising adult. Some children are liked by classmates despite this behavior. But for others, this behavior damages their reputation.

In order to help you understand why one child is liked and the other disliked, I'll describe two children I have known who talk back to their teacher. In the examples below, both are working on sand painting in the same classroom:

Talking back but has friends

> *Nick, age nine, makes frequent remarks that make fun of what the supervising adult tells him to do. The other children laugh at his comments: (To the instructor): "If we make that sand painting, can we go on vacation" (To another child trying to draw the sun in his picture): "That's a nice pinwheel you made."*
>
> *He does his own version of sand painting, sprinkling sand all over the paper. He starts horsing around with another child, both throwing a little sand on each other while smiling. Nick horses around several times each hour. Each time, the supervising adult tells him to stop. Each time, he listens to the adult by the second or third request.*

Nick is a minor pain in the neck to the supervising adult, but he helps to make the activity more enjoyable for the other children. I've known some adults who are very tolerant of children (some teachers are my super-heroes in this regard), and some adults who should never be around any child. Some teachers are well suited to teach classrooms of reasonably behaved children, but fly apart when they have a child who constantly talks back. Nick doesn't get along with some of his teachers.

Talking back and friendless

> *Monty, age nine, makes frequent belittling comments about the supervising adult's instructions. Typical comments are: "That's stupid," "That's boring," or "I don't want to do that." When the time comes to work on the craft, he is unsure what to do, and frequently demands help while the supervising adult is busy helping another child.*
>
> *While reaching for some glue, another child accidentally bumps him. His angry response is, "You messed up my work; now I'm going to mess up yours." He*

then throws sand at the other child and his project. The other child becomes upset.

The child who talks back to adults puts you in an awful position. Through no fault of your own, you find yourself talking to an adult who is upset about your child's behavior. You want his understanding and cooperation not his anger.

When an adult complains to you, you should have two objectives: work together with the complaining adult and help your child stop the offensive behavior. In this chapter I will tell you what to do when your child talks back. The next chapter will give you some additional help if your child is getting into physical fights with other children.

SOLVING THE PROBLEM:
Working together with a complaining adult

What do you do? You reassure the adult that you will help him with the problem. Here's how:

Step 1: Talk to the complaining adult.

Talking to the complaining adult may begin to defuse the situation.

Kathy, age nine, is in an after-school swim program. She constantly gets into trouble with the lifeguard for horsing around in the pool. Finally the lifeguard has had enough. He tells her he is never going allow her in the pool. From now on, she must sit on the sidelines and watch other children enjoying themselves.

Kathy's defiance frustrates the lifeguard. Up until now Kathy's parents have not spoken to the lifeguard. Without anywhere to turn, he takes drastic action.

Kathy's mom or dad should call the lifeguard and defuse this situation by following these guidelines:

1. *Be polite.* Check if you are talking to the adult at a good time for him.

2. *Stay calm.*

3. *Ask for specifics.* Ask for the adult's side of the issue, whether or not you think your child was at fault. The adult has important information you haven't heard.

4. *Express your concern about the issue* and your availability to work together with the adult.

5. *Arrange to keep communication open.* This is the best way you show that you are taking the problem seriously and you are not leaving the supervising adult alone to work on it.

Kathy's dad makes the call:

> *Dad:*   Hello, this is Kathy's dad. Is this a good time for you to talk?
>
> *Lifeguard:* Yes. I've been wanting to talk to you about Kathy. That girl has serious problems.

The lifeguard's complaint is out of proportion to what Kathy has done. He is clearly frustrated. Dad should stay calm and ask for specifics:

> *Dad:*   What has she been doing?
>
> *Lifeguard:* When the kids get into the pool, she starts horsing around and mouths off to me when I tell her to stop. I have 15 other children to supervise and I can't be playing policeman just for her.
>
> *Dad:*   I realize you have the safety of all of the children in mind. Is there anything I can do to help?
>
> *Lifeguard:* Kathy needs to listen to me the first time I tell her.
>
> *Dad:*   I agree. I will have a talk with her. Can I get daily reports from you on whether she listens?
>
> *Lifeguard:* That sounds good.
>
> *Dad:*   Great! I'll ask you each time I pick her up. Any time she doesn't listen to you I will take away a privilege when she gets home. I think she'll get the message if we both work together.

Dad's suggestion makes the lifeguard less angry at Kathy. This gives the lifeguard an alternative to permanently excluding her.

Step 2: Get your child to talk about the troublesome incident.

Kathy's dad asks for her view of the incident with the lifeguard. He does this to help her plan what she will do the next time this happens. He says nothing supportive of what she did (unless she describes ways she tried avoid conflict). He follows these guidelines when talking to Kathy:

1. *Don't accuse your child of being in the wrong.* This will get you nowhere and make it difficult for your child to continue the conversation.

2. *Don't say anything disrespectful about the adult.* Be a model of respect towards this adult, even if the adult is wrong. Always give the adult the benefit of the doubt, except if the adult is physically hurting or verbally abusing your child.

Here's how it's done:

Dad:	The lifeguard tells me you weren't listening to him today.
Kathy:	He accused me of something I didn't do.
Dad:	What did he say?
Kathy:	He said I was holding Kelsey's head under the water.
Dad:	Were you and what did you say?
Kathy:	I said, "I did not! You always blame me for things that other kids do!"
Dad:	Saying that got you kicked out of the pool. What would you do differently next time?
Kathy:	But he was wrong!
Dad:	If you want to keep swimming in the pool, you'll have to listen to him.
Kathy:	But he was wrong!
Dad:	He is an adult and you need to show respect for an adult.

Step 3: Have your child think of better ways to handle the incident.

Your main task is to have your child think of better ways to handle the problem. There are three rules your child should follow in this situation:

1. Explain the situation to the adult only once.

2. If this doesn't work, stop talking, even if you think the adult is wrong.

3. Don't get angry, answer back, give dirty looks or roll your eyes. An adult won't listen if you're disrespectful.

When you discuss the incident with your child:

Don't dispute your child's side of the story or make your child "tell the truth." This will take you off track. You will never know the truth. What matters most is that your child doesn't repeat the offense again.

Don't lecture. Your child will tune you out after you say the first few words anyway.

Kathy's dad teaches her these rules so she won't talk back:

Dad:	Next time the lifeguard accuses you, I want you to explain yourself only once, then stop talking and be respectful. Let's pretend I'm the lifeguard and I just thought I saw you dunking your friend's head under water. "Stop that. Out of the pool for five minutes." What are you going to do?
Kathy:	But I didn't do it.
Dad:	So what do you say to the lifeguard?
Kathy:	I didn't do it, but I'll stay out for 5 minutes.
Dad:	Good! Then what would you do?
Kathy:	Stay out for 5 minutes.
Dad:	That's great. I like that you told your side only once and didn't argue. Also, show me how you would look at the lifeguard when you are talking.
Kathy:	[*Looks with straight face*]

Dad: Good. You're not making any faces. Try it out next time it happens. If you listen to him next time, even if you think he was wrong, you won't get into more trouble. Tell me what happens.

Secure a promise from your child to do this next time.

Step 4: Give an immediate, brief penalty after each instance of talking back to an adult.

You make your point effectively when you give your child a brief penalty after each instance of talking back to the adult:

1. *The penalty should be brief,* no longer than 1-2 hours. The idea is *not* to make the penalty fit the crime, but to make the penalty just strong enough so your child will not repeat the behavior. You are looking for a steady decrease in talking back (for example from once a week to once every two weeks), so that after a few penalties, your child is no longer talking back. *Never use any kind of physical response that will cause your child pain as a penalty.*

2. *Penalty time should not be fun.* No games, TV, pleasant conversation, team sport, scout meeting, etc. If there is a movie you were planning to go to, it's canceled. If your child had a play date, make the penalty last until the play date (otherwise you're punishing the guest). If the play date will start too soon, give the penalty after the play date.

3. *State the exact penalty before beginning it,* for example, "I'm glad we came up with something better for you to try next time. But for now, you are grounded until 6 p.m. No TV or games until then."

4. *After the penalty is over, do not discuss it further.* Wipe the slate clean. *Don't* ask for an apology from your child. Sometimes children feel that an apology makes it okay to repeat the behavior again. This is a mistake. The only way things get better is *not* to repeat the behavior.

Give this penalty every time your child gets in trouble, including the first time. Most children will accept a penalty for behavior they know is not acceptable.

Step 5: Check back with the complaining adult.

Keep track of the number of incidents by getting daily or weekly reports from the complaining adult. If the number amounts to several each week, keep track of weekly totals.

Plan A: If weekly totals decrease:
Congratulations! Keep it up. You're on the right track!

Plan B: If weekly totals increase or stay the same:
If this happens for three weeks, seek professional help.

This is a lot to remember, so I have put this together into the checklist on the next page.

THE NEXT STEP:

Congratulations! Talking back to adults is a difficult problem to deal with. As with other trying times of being a parent, your patience and persistence has paid off. If your child is fighting with others, read the next chapter.

✔	Checklist for Working With Adults Who Have Trouble with Your Child

Step 1:	Talk to the complaining adult.
	    Be polite.
	    Stay calm.
	    Express your concern about the issue.
	    Ask for specifics.
	    Arrange to keep communication open.

Step 2:	Get your child to talk about the troublesome incident.
	    Don't accuse your child of being in the wrong.
	    Don't say anything disrespectful about the adult.

Step 3:	Have your child think of better ways to handle the incident.
	    Do secure a promise from your child to do this next time.
	    Don't make your child "tell the truth."
	    Don't lecture.

Step 4:	Give an immediate, brief penalty after each instance of talking back.
	    The penalty should be brief, no longer than 1-2 hours.
	    Penalty time should not be fun.
	    State the exact penalty before beginning it.
	    Never use any kind of physical response that will cause your child
	        pain as a penalty.
	    After the penalty is over, do not discuss it further. Wipe the slate
	        clean.

Step 5:	Check back with the complaining adult.
	    Plan A: If weekly totals decrease:
	        Keep it up, you're on the right track!
	    Plan B: If weekly totals increase or stay the same:
	        If this happens for three weeks, seek professional help.

26
STOPPING YOUR CHILD'S FIGHTING

THE PROBLEM:

The teacher says my child fights at school, but I don't see this at home. What's going on and what should I do?

How can I stop my child from getting into physical fights?

BACKGROUND: Children who fight

Six-year-old Jimmy has no friends in school. One time he is waiting to use the classroom computer with Andy, his classmate. Jimmy leans on Andy while he is waiting. Jimmy has done this before to Andy. Andy has seen other children having trouble with Jimmy. In his frustration, he screams at Jimmy to get away from him. Jimmy steps on Andy's foot hard as he is leaving and Andy begins to cry. This is the third child Jimmy has hurt this week and the teacher sends him to the principal.

The principal calls Jimmy's parents and tells them what has been happening. On the way home, Jimmy tells

*his version of what happened. "Andy was mean to me for no
reason and when I tried to get away from him, I
accidentally stepped on his foot."*

Jimmy's parents make the mistake of believing Jimmy's version
of what happened, despite the fact that he has hurt several other
children. They do nothing more about it. Jimmy hurts whoever
irritates him but is not aware that he irritates his classmates. He is
aware that no one likes him and that the kids tease him and pick on
him. His parents are not aware of what Jimmy does to provoke
others.

Children outgrow many behaviors, but fighting gets worse with
age. Some parents tell me, "I was like this when I was younger and I
turned out okay." Studies show the child who fights is at higher risk
for later serious social problems, such as delinquency and school
drop-out. The evidence is clear that you must discourage physical
fighting.

Some parents tell me they are painfully aware of their child's
fighting, but don't think there is anything they can do about it.
When parents see fighting as a serious problem and follow the next
steps, they can help their child to stop fighting.

SOLVING THE PROBLEM:
Helping your child find better ways to solve problems

Most fighting I hear about does not occur when parents are
watching. Parents hear about it from complaining adults and from
their child. The basic steps are the same as in the last chapter, but
you need more help for handling your child's fighting.

Step 1: Listen to the complaining adult.

Children who fight don't usually tell their parents about it,
especially if they get into trouble. The first time you hear of it is
when you are told by an adult who is supervising your child.

Sometimes, parents of a child who fights tell me their child
doesn't fight at home. For this reason, the parents have trouble
believing it is a real problem. They think:

◆ Maybe the other children are starting the fights and their child is striking back in self-defense.

◆ Maybe the teacher is picking on their child because the teacher doesn't like their child. This seems plausible, since teachers may get angry at a child who fights because teachers feel helpless to control it and feel an obligation to protect victims of fighting.

◆ Maybe it's normal for boys to get into fights. In fact, only 5-10% of boys get into fights.

Your first and most important step is to listen to the complaining adult. Follow the guidelines in Step 1 of the last chapter to deal effectively with the complaining adult. Acknowledge the problem and agree to work with the adult until it is no longer a problem. Example:

Teacher: Your son hit George Mayberry this morning.
Mom: What happened?
Teacher: I didn't see it start, but this is the third child John hit this week.
Mom: I'm surprised. He doesn't fight at home. He's going to be grounded tonight for it.
Teacher: I should think so.
Mom: I want this to stop. Can I get a report from you each day after school? Anytime I find he has hit someone, I will ground him. I want him to get the message that what he is doing is wrong.

Step 2: Get your child to talk about the troublesome incident.

As in the last chapter, listen to your child's side of the incident. You are doing this for three reasons. You want:

1. Your child to be clear on why he is being grounded.

2. To make it clear that there are no good excuses for fighting

3. Him to think of other things he can do instead of fighting.

Don't support any justification he gives, unless it was about an attempt to avoid fighting. Here's how you begin:

Mom: Your teacher told me you got into a fight with George at school today.

John: He started it.

Mom: What happened?

John: I was minding my own business. Out of nowhere, George came over and took my ball away. I didn't hurt him, I just got my ball back.

Don't get side tracked by disputing your child's side of the story. You are getting your child to start thinking about the situation which led to the fight.

Step 3: Have your child think of better ways to handle the incident.

Have your child to think of better ways to handle the problem. Here are some examples:

Better solutions to provocations

Another child...	Next time, you first...
is playing with a toy he doesn't know is yours.	tell him that it's yours.
frequently takes away a ball or toy of yours.	Younger children - tell an adult Older children - show no reaction (they're just trying to get you upset).
teases you.	use the "Make fun of the teasing" technique (Chapter 18).
hits, pushes you.	stay out of arm's reach. hang around with other kids. stay near the yard monitor.
barges in on a group game.	let the other kids handle it.

Two rules to enforce:

1. *Don't accept any reason for fighting.*

   The most common excuse I hear children give for fighting

is someone else started it. Self-defense is no excuse. Studies show that children who fight often mistake accidents for provocations. Parents tell me their children stop fighting when they don't accept any excuse for fighting.

2. *Don't allow you child to watch other children fighting.* The other common excuse I hear children use is that they weren't involved in the fight, they were just watching or trying to break up a fight between other children. This is a job for an adult. If your child is anywhere near a fight, you know he is in the wrong. You don't have to ask a lot of questions and it's easy to enforce.

John's mom teaches John to avoid fights:

Mom:	Fighting is never acceptable. What will you do the next time George takes your ball?
John:	But it's my ball. He can't have it!
Mom:	But fighting is wrong. What else will you do?
John:	I won't touch him. I'll just go away.
Mom:	I'm glad you won't touch him. You don't have to go away, but don't do anything, and see how long he keeps it before he gets tired of having it. He is probably trying to get you angry.
John:	Okay.

This discussion with John will not be enough to stop fighting.

Step 4: Give an immediate, brief penalty for each instance of fighting.

As in the last chapter, use these guidelines for the penalty. Remember:

1. *The penalty should be brief*, no longer than 1-2 hours.

2. *The penalty should not be fun.* No games, TV, pleasant conversation, team sport, scout meeting, etc. If there is a movie you were planning on going to, it's canceled. If your child had a play date, make the penalty last until the play date (otherwise you're punishing the guest). If the play date

starts too soon, give the penalty after the play date. *Never use any kind of physical response that will cause your child pain as a penalty.*

3. *State the exact penalty before beginning it,* for example, "I'm glad we came up with something better for you to try next time. But for now, you are grounded until 6 p.m. No TV or games until then."

4. *After the penalty is over, do not discuss it further.* Don't ask for an apology from your child.

Give this penalty every time your child gets in trouble, including the first time. Keep track of the number of fights your child gets into. The following checklist puts this all together for you.

THE NEXT STEP:

Fighting is a difficult problem to work on. You deserve a lot of credit for seeing this through. Fighting not only interferes with friendships but sometimes leads to more serious problems in adolescence. If your child's fighting has damaged his reputation, read Chapter 24. Then you can go to Parts II and III to get the help your child needs to make and keep friends.

✔	Checklist for stopping physical fighting

Step 1:	Listen to the complaining adult.
	    Be polite.
	    Stay calm.
	    Express your concern about the issue.
	    Ask for specifics.
	    Arrange to keep communication open.

Step 2:	Get your child to talk about the troublesome incident.
	    Don't accuse your child of being in the wrong.
	    Don't say anything disrespectful about the adult.
	    Don't accept any reason for fighting.
	    Don't allow you child to watch other children fighting.

Step 3:	Have your child think of better ways to handle the incident .
	    Do secure a promise from your child to do this next time.
	    Don't make your child "tell the truth."
	    Don't lecture.

Step 4:	Give an immediate, brief penalty after each instance of fighting.
	    The penalty should be brief, no longer than 1-2 hours.
	    Penalty time should not be fun.
	    State the exact penalty before beginning it.
	    Never use any kind of physical response that will cause your child
	        pain as a penalty.
	    After the penalty is over, do not discuss it further. Wipe the slate
	        clean.

Step 5:	Check back with the complaining adultt.
	    Plan A: If fights decrease each week:
	        Keep it up, you're on the right track!
	    Plan B: If fightts increase or stay the same each week:
	        If this happens for three weeks, seek professional help.

27
STOPPING YOUR CHILD'S BULLYING

THE PROBLEM:
How can I stop my child from being cruel to others?

BACKGROUND: Common Patterns of Bullying

The principal calls you in for a conference about your child. She tells you your child and his friend have been taunting and scaring a younger girl. This is how parents most often discover their child has been bullying. All you knew up to this point was that your child had a circle of friends. You had doubts about some of these friends, but nothing serious enough for you to act on.

A bully is cruel to a specific child over a long period of time. Bullying groups usually have a leader, who is physically stronger than most others his age. There are usually one or two followers, who don't lead attacks on others but enjoy watching them or help come up with new ideas. If the child being bullied is disliked by classmates, more children may join in the bullying group. Your child's bullying is not a reflection on you, but an indication that:

1. Your child has nothing better to do with his time.

2. He has fallen in with the wrong circle of friends.

SOLVING THE PROBLEM: How to stop bullying

Eliminate both of these reasons for bullying as follows:

Step 1: Do not support bullying.

Nothing justifies bullying, even if the victim is disliked by most others. Give your child the clear message that what he did was wrong:

> *Dad:* Your principal tells me that you've been bothering a younger girl every day at recess.
>
> *Tyler:* She's always annoying the rest of the kids and I don't really bother her.
>
> *Dad:* You have no reason to be near a younger girl.

Step 2: Give your child six simple rules to prevent bullying.

Surgically remove that portion of your child's life that was devoted to bullying. If the school Principal has complained to you about bullying, reassure her that you are taking action. Make sure that the school will also supervise your child. Simple rules need less detective work and are easily enforced. Here's what you tell your child:

1. Stay away from the child you picked on.

2. You are not allowed to hang out with the children who were bullying with you.

3. Go directly to school and come directly home from school. (These are prime times for bullying.)

4. When you invite children over, play only on our property so that I know where you are at all times.

5. You are not allowed to visit someone else's house before I meet him and his parents.

6. When you go to someone else's house, you need to stay where his parent can see you at all times.

Here's how Dad tells these rules to Tyler:

Dad: From now on, the girl you were annoying is off limits to you. You are not to be within 20 feet of her and are not to talk to her. Do you understand?

Tyler: That's not fair!

Dad: There's no excuse for bothering her.

Tyler: I don't bother her.

Dad: Then it should be easy for you to do what I said. Since the principal told me that Andy was doing this with you, you are not to play with Andy. Since this happened on the way to school, I will be driving you to school until you show us we can trust you again.

Children like Tyler will be quietly resigned to the restrictions after parents and teachers become involved. A soon-to-be former bully usually sees that what he did is wrong and that this restriction is just. Dad has corrected a potential character flaw.

Step 3: Check on your child's activities outside your home.

Before accepting an invitation for a play date, always tell the host's parent that one of your rules is that your child be supervised at all times (you don't have to say why). After the play date, always ask the host's parent about the activities of the play date. Here's how Tyler's mom questions Dylan's mom:

Mom: Was Tyler okay?

Dylan's Mom: He was okay.

Mom: What did they do?

Dylan's Mom: They shot some hoops out in the back yard.

Mom: What else did they do?

Dylan's Mom: They hung out in the tree house.

Mom: That must have been fun.

If Dylan's mom didn't know what they were doing or let them go somewhere unsupervised, then steer Tyler away from Dylan.

Step 4: Provide an immediate, brief penalty after one of the rules is broken.
Remember these guidelines:

1. Don't or use any kind of physical response as a penalty.
Remember, you're teaching that physical intimidation is never acceptable.

2. Don't restrict other aspects of your child's life.
You want him to acquire more productive interests. Never take away a play date with another child who doesn't bully.

3. Select a penalty you can enforce.
If your child has damaged another child's belongings, take away two or three weeks of his allowance to pay for part of it. It is not necessary for your child to totally repay the damage (although you need to offer to totally compensate the family of the injured child). Other appropriate penalties are restriction in TV time for the evening or missing a movie your child was planning to see.

4. Give it immediately after you find out a rule has been broken.

5. State the exact penalty before beginning it. Examples:

Mom:	Since you destroyed that child's backpack, I'll pay your allowance for the next two weeks to him.
	-or-
Mom:	Since I saw you standing next to Alan and you weren't supposed to go near him, there will be no TV tonight.
	-or-
Mom:	You left the backyard when you were not supposed to. There will be no TV tonight.

6. After the penalty is over, do not discuss it further
and wipe the slate clean.

Step 5: Keep track of rule violations.

If your child frequently breaks the rules you have set up, continue to impose penalties, but consider seeking professional help.

THE NEXT STEP:

You deserve a lot of credit for dealing with your child's bullying. Children who bully have fallen in with the wrong crowd. This crowd can sometimes lead them into more serious trouble as they get older. Read Chapters 12 and 13 to help your child to select new friends to replace the children who were bullying with him.

CLOSING THOUGHT

You have taught your child skills which will
last a lifetime. I hope that in addition to
helping your child, that you have enjoyed
learning about how the roots of adult social
behavior spring from our childhood.

SUGGESTED READING

Barkley, R. *Defiant Children*. New York: Guilford Press.

Cole, M., & Cole, S.R. *The Development of Children*. New York: W.H. Freeman, 1993.

Olweus, D. *Bullying at School: What we know and what we can do*. Cambridge: Blackwell Publishers, 1993.

Orenstein, P., in association with the American Association of University Women. *Schoolgirls: Young women, self-esteem, and the confidence gap*. New York: Doubleday, 1994.

Whitham, C. *Win the Whining War and Other Skirmishes*. Los Angeles: Perspective Publishing, 1991.

Zimbardo, P. G. *The Shy Child: A parent's guide to preventing and overcoming shyness from infancy to adulthood*. New York: McGraw-Hill, 1981.

INDEX

Order Form

Send to: Perspective Publishing, Inc.
50 S. DeLacey Ave., Suite 201
Pasadena, CA 91105 • 818/440-9635

Win the Whining War & Other Skirmishes

This easy-to-use guide helps parents increase cooperation and reduce conflict with children ages 2-12. Step-by-step, parents learn how to cut out all the annoying behavior (tantrums, teasing, dawdling, interrupting, complaining, etc.) that drives them crazy.

___ copies @ $13.95 Total $_____

"The Answer is NO": Saying it and sticking to it

In this sequel to Win the Whining War & Other Skirmishes, author Cynthia Whitham tackles twenty-six situations that plague parents of 2-12 year-olds. From bedtime to pets, makeup to music, homework to designer clothes, Whitham helps parents define their values, build good parenting habits, and set firm, fair limits.

___ copies @ $13.95 Total $_____

Survival Tips for Working Moms : 297 REAL Tips from REAL Moms

Full of examples of how the tips actually work in real families, this is a light but no-nonsense practical resource thast can help every working mom. From chores to childcare, errands to exercise, this book makes life easier. Almost 100 cartoons make this a book you can't put down.

___ copies @ $10.95 Total $_____

The Invasion of Planet Wampetter

by Samuel H. Pillsbury, illustrated by Matthew Angorn
Ages 8 and up; hardback
Young Wampetters Gartrude and Eloise Tub lead a desparate effort to thwart a plan by human developers to turn their planet into a galctic tourist trap.

___ copies @ $15.00 Total $_____

Good Friends Are Hard to Find

___ copies @ $13.95 Total $_____

Subtotal: _____
Shipping: _____ Please add $3.50 for first book, .50 for each additional book.
Sales Tax: _____ California residents add 8.25% sales tax
TOTAL ENCLOSED: _____

Name: _____

Address: _____

_____

Phone: (_____)_____

Or use a credit card and order toll free 1-800-330-5851